ENDORSEMENTS

There Must Be More is a must read for anyone whose hunger for authentic Christianity is greater than their comfort. Keith writes with an honesty and frankness that is both refreshing and challenging. This book is real, because the author is. As you read through Keith's journey you will be drawn into an intense longing for all the joy, peace and righteousness God provides for all who are born into His kingdom - and you won't be disappointed in the experience. *There Must Be More* should have a warning label: "Reading this book will cause great damage to religious bondage." I'm honored to endorse this book and to call Keith my friend.

David Crone, Senior Leader of The Mission, Author of *Decisions That Define Us* and *The Power Of Your life Message*

To read Keith's book is to encounter reality. He opens up his own life and journey in a way that is disarming. But, alongside the honesty, passion comes through the pages in equal measure. Those twin characteristics are joined together in such a way that the very reading of the book leaves a hunger for an experience of the same reality. Not simply the same experience, for this is Keith's story and his experience; but a desire for something that is not borrowed from someone else, but is deeply personal and real. The message of the Gospels and Keith's message is that very real encounter is there for each of us. Recommended? Absolutely. Read, walk through the door of honesty and let the inner passion for 'more' draw you and the Living Christ together.

Martin Scott
Author of *Gaining Ground* and *Impacting The City*

I've walked with Keith Ferrante through many of the years written about in this book and have first hand experience in witnessing his transition. There are helpful insights that come from life experience and Keith has put a string of nuggets together in *There Must Be More*. If you want to shed a life of religious practice and expectation to find freedom in your promise of abundant life, then I recommend that you read his book.

Danny Silk
Sr. Leadership Team Bethel Church, Redding CA
President of Loving On Purpose
Author of *Culture of Honor* and *Loving Our Kids On Purpose*

It is a real honor to write a recommendation for *There Must Be More...* a candid and transparent look at a young Revivalist as he journeys from religious bondage to Kingdom destiny. Having known Keith and Heather Ferrante, and having been a part of their journey for over twelve years, I can tell you from first hand experience that Keith carries true revival fire. I have watched him grow from a young, hungry pastor into a great father who walks with wisdom and maturity beyond his years.

This book will challenge your thinking and communicate reformation strategies designed to bring on a fresh move of God. Keith Ferrante is the new breed of Kingdom Revivalist that was prophesied to come many years ago and I am privileged to recommend Keith and very proud to call him son!

Wendell McGowan/Prophetic Revivalist
www.wendellmcgowan.org

Keith Ferrante has one of the strongest gifts of personal prophetic encouragement that I know. He has an unusual ability to stir hope and vision in lives through his anointed and powerful words. *There Must Be More* is an overflow of his life and this gift. In this empowering book, Keith opens up his life to share his story of experiencing the "more" of God. You will relate to his journey of overcoming fear, rejection and man pleasing. Your faith will grow as you read his revelation about the finished work of the cross and about who we are in Him. Get ready to be ignited with hope and courage to experience God like never before – and then sharing it with others in ways you never thought you could. Bravo, Keith. You are a blessing to the body of Christ.

Steve Backlund – Ignited Hope Ministries
Bethel Global Legacy Leadership Team

There Must Be
MORE

A Journey To Freedom

By Keith Ferrante

Published by Dream Chasers Media Group, LLC
Las Vegas, NV
info@dreamchasersmedia.com

Cover Designer: Pamela Trush for Delaney-Designs

Library of Congress Control Number: 2012933400

ISBN-13: 978-0-9817581-6-9
ISBN-10: 0-9817581-6-9

Dedication

To my children, Maci and Micah – *This book is dedicated to you.*
My prayer is that you and the generations to come would take the
freedom we fought to gain and show us what growing up free can
look like. I pray that you both would affect your generation.

Acknowledgements

Willits Shiloh Gateway of Worship – Without your friendship, partnership, love, and belief in me this book would not have been written. You walked with me through this process of transitioning from an old wineskin into the new. Thank you!! You will always be family.

Kris Vallotton, David and Deborah Crone, Wendell McGowan, Wes Crone, Rich and Lindy Oliver, Dan McCollam, Steve and Wendy Backlund, Martin Scott, Georgian Banov, and a few others. You were the mentors that personally spoke into my life and each brought a significant part to my journey into freedom. I am forever grateful.

Madeline Guzzo – Thank you so much for your tireless effort to take my writings and help make it a book.

Ron and Cheri Gollner and the Dream Chasers Media Group team – Thank you so much for your finishing touches on this book. You took it much further than you had to. May God richly bless you.

Mom and Dad – You have given me a rich heritage that I am forever grateful for. You prayed that I would affect my generation. The changes that the Lord brought in me are a part of your prayers. My love for you both is inexpressible.

To my lovely wife Heather – You believed in me even when I was full of fear and control. You walked with me through the journey. You forgave me countless times for too many things to count. Without you I would not be here today. Thank you for being the most amazing wife a man could ask for.

Table of Contents

Foreword

There Must Be More is Keith Ferrante's epic journey into a deeper relationship with the Creator of the world. Unlike many books I've read on this subject, Keith's book is a gut wrenching, honest and insightful account of his rite of passage out of the clutches of stale religion and into God's great adventure.

Keith's transparency is disarming and refreshing. *There Must Be More,* hews out a path through the snake infested jungle of self-righteous and pious thinking. This book is a treasure map setting a clear course for all those that are sick of mere religious form and are hungry for more of God.

I have personally mentored Keith and Heather Ferrante for over ten years. When I first met Keith he was like a beautiful, yet wild stallion. His passion and strength were exciting to watch from a distance but being in a "corral" with him was risky business. A religious spirit had sucked the life out of the culture around him and imprisoned his zeal for God. Much like Saul of Tarsus, his need for justice was harming the Believers around him. Keith's heart was pure yet he was completely unaware of how the people around him experienced him. Keith describes in great detail his own painful path into an incredible spiritual awakening that transformed him from an offensive, bored Christian to a vibrant and virtuous leader.

Keith also unearths ancient Kingdom virtues that were somehow buried in the sands of time. Virtues like loyalty, honor and accountability are dispersed through the pages of this book to equip the Body of Christ to live powerfully and create a healthy culture. This culture invites new and deeper expressions of the manifest presence of God in, on and through His noble people.

Keith leaves clear and insightful markers on this path so that his readers can follow his personal pilgrimage into deeper dimensions of God. If you feel discouraged, powerless or just bored this book is for you. *There Must Be More*, will challenge your perspectives, rock your realities and transform your life. I highly recommend this book to every Christian.

Kris Vallotton

Co-Founder of Bethel School of Supernatural Ministry
Author of seven books including, *The Supernatural Ways of Royalty*
Senior Associate Leader of Bethel Church, Redding, California

Introduction

If you picked up this book I believe the Lord ordained you to read it. It is a book that will free you from the chains of traditions grown cold and transform your heart's once frigid landscape into one of blazing passion.

This book is my journey out of the bondage of religion, through the desert of change, and into the promised land of God's blessings. It is my journey and perspective of the events of my life. Others may have regarded these events differently and I am certain their views are valid.

My experiences and conclusions are not meant to belittle situations or people involved in my life. They are revealed to offer you a context of how my freedom came about. Individuals draw their own unique conclusions in life, and for that we are incredibly thankful. I would like to share my revelations, and hope that they help you gain greater realms of freedom in your personal circumstances and life story.

I am tremendously thankful for the rich heritage passed on to me by my parents, grandparents, and legacy of spiritual leaders. Without their enormous sacrifices I would not have expanded the spiritual borders of the promised lands entrusted to me. I am confident the prayers of my parents and grandparents—that I would affect my generation—are coming to pass today. I pray that my journey into unknown lands to expand a spiritual legacy will prompt you to embrace the privilege of increasing your spiritual borders.

In the midst of acquiring a spiritual legacy from my family I discovered there was more freedom to be had, but to realize this freedom I would have to journey farther than the lands of blessing I had already inherited. I felt that to see the "Kingdoms of this world become the Kingdom of our God" in my scope of influence, I must first escape the confines of my present circumstances. By God's grace

He showed me the way out when I was not even looking for it and for that I am forever grateful. To all those who paid a dear price to help me obtain greater freedom, I dedicate this book.

May all who read the pages of this book find the freedom I found, and may you be compelled to lead others out of bondage into His glorious light.

Forever indebted to Christ,

Keith Ferrante

Chapter 1

There Must be More

I grew up in church; I bet I was born under a pew. From day one I attended every function, service, prayer meeting—you name it. I was saved at four years old and have been preaching ever since. My first sermon as a preschooler occurred at my grandparents' house. We were playing church. My two brothers facilitated the offering and announcements, and I preached.

The first sermon went something like this: "There is God, there is Jesus, and there's Grover."

Now church was a serious matter to us; and my brothers were unsure if I should share so comically about God. We sheepishly glanced at my grandparents to see their reaction, and when they smiled we all burst into laughter. God, Jesus and Sesame Street's Grover...what a good first attempt.

At the age of seven, I was filled with the Holy Spirit at a Christian summer camp and spoke in tongues all night long. The camp counselors had to shake me out of my state of spiritual ecstasy so I could get some rest. I was very zealous for the Lord, passionate to tell people about Jesus. I led my first person to the Lord in the upright monster truck tire on our elementary school playground. Later that day when my first convert rode the school bus home, he publicly questioned everyone if they knew his new friend, Jesus. During the elementary years I carried my Bible to school and preached to my teachers, who referred me to school counselors, convinced that I was a spiritual fanatic.

Well...they were right!

My mom believed that I was unusually in tune with the Lord for a child my age. I spent hours in my bedroom closet, squished between hanging clothes, zealously speaking in tongues. Sometimes my friends made fun of me, but that did not dampen my passion to serve Jesus, for I felt that one's beliefs and actions should not be compromised. To not talk about Jesus or actively demonstrate my faith would be to deny the one who unashamedly gave His life for me.

My parents instilled in me the value of studying the Word of God. Our daily routine included reading several chapters of scripture and journaling things that were particularly meaningful, memorizing many verses and learning numerous stories along the way. I am so thankful for this powerful inheritance from my parents and extended family.

My passion was fanned into flame by my maternal grandfather. Each year during the summer, I spent a week or two at his home. Grandpa and Grandma modeled the importance of prayer and fasting. Their day began and ended with prayer and the Word. These experiences increased my already burning desire to "sell out" my life for Christ.

I enrolled in a reputable Bible College in anticipation of furthering the legacy of my father and paternal grandfather. Those who followed this path were highly esteemed in my church and family circles. Although I passionately pursued this course, something in my heart cried out, "God, there must be more." Little did I know what that *more* would cost and how it would transform my life.

As I studied the scriptures in young adulthood, I recognized that my life did not have the same power that I read about in the Bible stories. Something in my heart knew there must be more. Around this time, in the mid 1990's, a new move of God began to emerge. I was a Bible college student hearing from professors and students alike about manifestations of laughter, signs and wonders and extravagant, unrestrained worship. I had absolutely no grid for this. The new move of God raged onward, but I remained at a distance. Some of my professors believed that this movement was definitely not of God and I, myself, suspected that it might be dangerous.

"It's a cult!" "It's something to stay away from!" "This is definitely not for anyone of spiritual maturity!" All common claims from my professors, although several who migrated toward the "hot spots" of signs and wonders were radically changed. I, on the other hand, stayed as far away from the "weird" ones as I could.

During this time I met Heather Michelle Tolentino: fellow student... and my future wife. She and some of her girl friends had attended the Brownsville Revival in Pensacola, Florida and returned laughing for days and dancing wildly in worship. Not only were these manifestations completely foreign to me, my level of Biblical knowledge put them in the "of the flesh" category. I vividly recall seeing these girls laughing uncontrollably one lunch hour in the cafeteria while my "cool" guy friends and I looked on convinced that it was utter nonsense.

As students, we were required to attend chapel five days a week. We had a time of worship and then listened to a sermon, but certainly nothing outrageous ever occurred except a few pranks played by my friends. On one particular day I noticed a young lady in the aisle worshiping through dance. Let me stress that *nobody* danced at my school. On rare occasions I saw dancing during a church service, but it was only judged acceptable if it was God initiated, of the Spirit and involuntary. Now in front of my eyes here was a young lady boldly dancing her little jig for Jesus. Of course, it was Heather. When the appropriate time came, I did my Christian duty and zealously informed her that not only was she "in the flesh," but it was a sign of pride and no truly spiritual person would publicly dance in front of others. Sadly, my admonition was effective and Heather shut down her dance for several years.

Despite our unpleasant first interactions, within a year of meeting— and at the ripe old age of twenty-two—Heather and I married and shortly after found ourselves pastoring our first church in Willits, California. Willits, situated a few hours north of San Francisco, is known as the gateway to the Redwoods. My dad pastored in Willits for six years and another gentleman briefly pastored the same church after him. It was this pastor who recruited us to be youth pastors. We actually grew that youth group to around one hundred students. A few months after we came on staff, the pastor left the church and to our complete surprise, the membership voted for Heather and I to become their pastors.

The people the Lord gave me to pastor were the same people I had grown up with during my high school years. I loved them and they loved me. I was a young, sold-out Christian who caught their attention. With the help of a few others, I had led the youth group when I was 15 years old and experienced the first youth revival of this church. We had witnessed a few drug addicts and football players saved and set on fire by God.

Heather and I found favor with our regional denominational leaders and were encouraged to press toward greater levels of leadership. I maintained contact with these leaders and as the move of God grew, so did our disapproval of it. We actively looked for strategies to shut down this emerging outpouring. Our leaders encouraged us to use whatever realm of authority we possessed to tame this "dangerous expression of Christian experience." There were a few in our church who had been touched by this fledgling revival, but we renounced their testimonies as not being truly from God. In spite of our best efforts our church experienced an acceleration of hunger for more of the Lord — and more was on its way...but certainly not in a manner I could ever have anticipated.

It began on a hot summer day in the middle of July. Bill Johnson and David Crone were invited as guest speakers for a weeklong family camp sponsored by a group of affiliated churches. Bill was at the center of this "questionable" move of God, so prior to the gathering I had a phone conversation with him that was basically an interrogation. My view of Christianity prevented me from embracing Bill's revelation of God and almost thwarted his presence at the camp. Although I had authority to cancel his invitation, something inside of me would not allow it. Therefore, the leadership I served encouraged me to closely monitor the activities of these guests.

An uncanny thing happened that week. It was as if someone had painted a bull's eye on my chest. As I led worship, the guest ministers' teams approached to pray and prophesy over me, sharing details about my life only God knew. Mind you, I had no grasp of this type of pointed, yet edifying, prophecy. David Crone and his ministry team pulled my wife Heather and I into the prayer room one afternoon and proceeded to speak into our lives. I recall one prophecy in particular that truly convicted me, and that the Lord used over a period of a few years to transform my life.

"Keith, you have Heather on your arm like a hawk. You let her go and then she has to come back to your arm," one prophesied.

At that moment, the Lord convicted me of the control in which I operated and projected onto everyone in my life.

Throughout this week my life radically changed as Heather and I were completely blessed by these people. Something in me was awakened by the love of God flowing through these special messengers. They became channels through which Jesus Himself was being revealed. Even though I had previously rejected it, God saw my heart crying out for more and He dramatically answered my cry. There were many healings, prophecies and life-giving revelations at that camp in July; all of which were illustrations of this fresh move of God. These encounters were exhilarating, but the most significant change occurred inside of me...because others loved me unconditionally even though I had set my heart against them. That week I discovered the *more* of God that was waiting for me.

My first taste was love, and that is where my journey to freedom began.

Chapter 2

Papa's Hug

Amazing, unconditional love captured and drew me into something for which I had no paradigm. If you would have asked me if I knew the Father's love, I would have emphatically responded, "Yes." But, did I experientially know His love? No. I was not familiar with unconditional love. I was driven to please people. If I did not meet others' expectations, complete my tasks flawlessly, or think all the "right" thoughts, I internally beat myself up. Then I would try to work my way back into feelings of well being through fasting, prayer or being tough on myself.

I started every prayer with, "Father, forgive me, I am sure I have done something wrong." It was perplexing to me that the Lord's Prayer did not begin in this manner, because I assumed that is how we were supposed to approach His altar. I mean how could God possibly accept you without first ensuring that your internal sin slate was perfectly clean?

I was sin conscious, not God conscious.

I was scared of being punished by God and others. I was fearful that I would not hear, "Well done, Keith." I constantly analyzed my behaviors, thoughts and actions.

Did I preach with the right motive today?

Did I love that person enough?

Did I keep my thoughts pure?

Around and around I went on my internal merry-go-round.

Much like the Abraham Lincoln Memorial in Washington D.C., I pictured God sitting high on a cold and unapproachable throne, waiting to zap me with a lightning bolt if I made one mistake. Did I please Him? Was He angry with me? My salvation teetered and I was consumed with worry about my final Day of Judgment before the Lord.

I was good at receiving affection from my mother or other women, but receiving a hug from a male felt awkward and weird. As the Lord led me deeper into a journey of love, I had no idea how difficult it would be. An older gentleman, who became a model of the Father's love, invited me one day to an encounter with God.

Heather and I were attending a conference in Vacaville, California when a gentleman approached me. He said he felt that the Lord had something for me and invited me to join him in the prayer room if I wanted to receive it. I was skeptical and had no idea what I was getting into, but reluctantly followed him. When we entered the room he asked if he could pray over me while we embraced in a hug. It was awkward and uncomfortable for me, but during that time of prayer I had a vision. In that vision I watched as my heavenly Father sat on the floor and played Lego's™ with me. Growing up I loved to play with Lego's™. The vision was the start of a journey where the Lord revealed that He did not just forgive me of sins, but He actually loved and delighted in me. In fact, He was interested in the same things that interested me — a true father, passionately caring for and about His children.

One day in my thirties I had a childish thought — I suddenly wanted to hold and play with a child's bouncy ball. Later that same day, I visited my dad and he presented me with a bouncy ball, not exactly the kind of gift a father would give to his grown son. He had no idea of my childlike desire, but that simple little gift from my heavenly Father through my earthly father taught me that God cares about the simplest desires of our hearts.

Following this experience, I lost a screw for my motorcycle while replacing a broken part. After spending hours searching for it the Lord revealed its location and immediately I was able to track it down. As

I held that screw in the palm of my hand, the Lord gently said, "Son, I am as small as a screw and as big as anything you need." What a caring, loving God. I realized He was concerned about everything that caused me concern or worry, no matter how big or how small.

As time went on I continued to experience the Father's acceptance and affirmation in many ways. One day while worshiping the Lord on my guitar in the privacy of the prayer room at church, I sang to the Lord, "I love You Dad, I love You Dad..." Over and over I sang it. Audibly, I heard the Father sing back to me the same melody, "I love you son, I love you son..." as angels sang "Hallelujah" in the background. Overwhelmed by this unusual experience of hearing His audible voice I burst into tears and cried at the top of my lungs as the well of emotions hidden beneath my strong, outer veneer burst forth. Because I had a meeting to attend, I had to compose myself, but when I arrived home, the floodgates of emotions ruptured again. My daughter who was around four years old at the time remarked, "Daddy is a good crier, Mommy!" The Lord was softening my heart to His tender care, one encounter after another.

Later on that week at a men's camp during a ministry time, a brother gently shook me and said, "You are wound too tight and it is hard to receive that way...you need to relax!" It was true...I was like a brick wall. One thousand people could be slain under the power of God and I would be the only one standing. Releasing my emotional guard and my professional ministerial outer shell was not easy for me. I did not know how to receive tangible love. Yet, God was relentless.

As the individual began to pray for me, I relaxed my body and in that posture of surrender, the passion of God overwhelmed me and I fell to the ground. I felt a load lift from my shoulders and suddenly a revelation hit me: I could minister *to* others, but did not know how to receive *from* others. Once I saw how off kilter I was, I did not want to minister to another person again. I recognized the freedom of allowing the Lord — not me — to be the strong one. The gentleman ministering to me said, "Now that you are free to not minister, why don't you minister to a couple of those guys standing over there?" Because God had freed me from using ministry for validation, others were greatly impacted by my prayers that night.

The meetings I attended to feed my spiritual hunger were filled with expressions of worship, physical manifestations and styles of ministry unusual to me. For several years I found myself intellectually offended, thinking, "That can't be God; that is of the flesh; that is weird." As I drove home in frustration from one of these meetings the Lord gently whispered, "Son, the methods of ministry aren't sacred. The message is. So let go of the need to judge everyone."

There were so many things to deal with in my life. I was like an onion, continually peeled in an effort to reach the edible core. Regardless of the freedom I experienced, I still found myself striving to please God. One day while I was worshiping, He whispered, "Son, if you never sing for me again I will still love you until the end. My love for you is not based on your performance. Son, I accepted you unconditionally when you first gave your life to me at age four. My acceptance of you has never changed. Why are you trying so hard to please me when I have already approved of you?"

Wow. I did not realize I worked so hard to please the one who already delighted in me. His affirmation was not based on my performance, a perfect day or even how good or bad I felt. His love for me was based on the simple fact that He had accepted me in Christ. "Son," He gently reminded me, "I accepted Jesus before He had done one ounce of ministry."

Matthew 3:17 says it this way, *"And a voice from heaven said, 'This is my Son, whom I love; with him I am well pleased.'"* Learning to surrender and allow God to love me, regardless of my actions, was a difficult journey. It was His unconditional love that captured me, despite my blindness to His vast storehouse of grace and kindness. It was love that broke the barrier of my resistant heart and taught me how to feel. It was love that allowed me to enjoy who I am and in return enjoy others for who they are.

The prodigal son's story was my story. I used to presume the parable was only about the lost, but I did not realize how truly lost I was as a believer. I was lost because I had yet to encounter His love. I was like the prodigal son who ran away and finally returned saying, *"I will set out and go back to my father and say to him: Father, I have sinned against heaven and against you. I am no longer worthy to be called your son; make me like one of your hired men."* (Luke 15:18-19). I assumed that my sins, shortfalls and mistakes disqualified me from being a son with privileges. I felt on top of the world one day and unworthy the next. Do you ever feel unsure about where you stand with God?

God sent Jesus to die for us and to end that uncertainty once and for all. John 3:16 says, *"For God so loved the world that he gave his one and only Son, that whoever believes in him shall not perish but have eternal life."* I used to think that God could not look at me because of my uniqueness—my passion, my personality, both of which I thought were insufficient. I was not entrenched in sin, but I could not embrace myself as He did. My belief was that He had to send Jesus so he could behold me. In my eyes, my personality make-up was unacceptable. God could only view me through Jesus for full acceptance. I looked at Him through the wrong lens. He created me! John 3:16 notes, *"... [For God] so loved the world."* He so loved me while I was still a sinner. Romans 5:8 says, *"But God demonstrates his own love for us in this: While we were still sinners, Christ died for us."*

Do you ever think that God can only love you when you are doing well, ministering, touching many lives and striving hard for Him? Remember, the Bible says, *"While we were still sinners He loved us."* He did not send Jesus for His sake; He sent Jesus for our sake. He always loved us, but our sin caused us to run and hide from relationship with the Father--like Adam and Eve who hid the first time they disobeyed.

Genesis 3:8-10, *Then the man and his wife heard the sound of the Lord God as he was walking in the garden in the cool of the day, and they hid from the Lord God among the trees of the garden. But the Lord God called to the man, "Where are you?" He answered, "I heard you in the garden, and I was afraid because I was naked; so I hid.*

God sent Jesus to deal with our shame so we could boldly approach our Daddy without fear now or ever. 1 John 4:17-18 states, *In this way, love is made complete among us so that we will have confidence on the day of judgment, because in this world we are like him. There is no fear in love. But perfect love drives out fear, because fear has to do with punishment. The one who fears is not made perfect in love.*

I do not have to wonder anymore about Judgment Day for that day is not intended for me. It was settled in Christ. I can now have confidence all the way through Judgment Day knowing I am loved and accepted in Christ. Romans 15:7 says it this way, *"Accept one another, then, just as Christ accepted you, in order to bring praise to God."*

Many people still fear the Day of Judgment and hearing, "Well done" or, "Go away." They live striving to be morally presentable to God, carefully walking a tight rope of right and wrong. They do not realize that the Father took care of our right standing through Jesus. I do not have to walk the tightrope of moral standards to be pleasing to God. I am pleasing to God through Christ. Paul says it this way in Philippians 3:8-9, *What is more I consider everything a loss compared to the surpassing greatness of knowing Christ Jesus my Lord, for whose sake I have lost all things. I consider them rubbish, that I may gain Christ and be found in Him, not having a righteousness of my own that comes from the law, but that which is through faith in Christ – the righteousness that comes from God and is by faith.*

Jesus took on my sin, took my punishment, became a curse and subsequently set me in right relationship with God. I am not in right standing with God, or righteous as the result of good moral behavior, as important as it may be. I am forever pardoned—the beneficiary of continuous love and affection.

Romans 8:1-3, says, *Therefore, there is now no condemnation for those who are in Christ Jesus, because through Christ Jesus the law of the Spirit of life set me free from the law of sin and death. For what the law was powerless to do in that it was weakened by the sinful nature, God did by sending his own Son in the likeness of sinful man to be a sin offering. And so he condemned sin in sinful man.*

There is no condemnation or punishment for those who are in Christ Jesus. What good news! I am free of the fear of punishment. Now and forever. I can be disciplined, but that is a separate issue. The Message Bible says this: *God is educating you; that is why you must never drop out. He's treating you as dear children. This trouble you're in isn't punishment; it's training, the normal experience of children* (Hebrews 12:9).

Discipline is like a workout that fortifies me in an area in which I need to build spiritual muscle. Punishment is wrath poured out in anger. I need not live a life tiptoeing around the Father, trying to remain on His good side while avoiding His indignation. I know that I am forever approved in Christ and Christ lives in me. I am now free to pursue my destiny knowing the One who died for me lives inside of me and will help me display His victory in this life.

The revelation of the Father's love for me was an unfolding discovery, requiring many years to transform my mind and settle into my spirit. Shame and condemnation, fear of punishment and slavery to performance relentlessly stood their ground on the landscape of my heart. Through unconditional love they were eventually driven off. I am thankful for the graciousness of my heavenly Father. In the next chapter I will unfold the process of how the heavenly Father, through earthly spiritual fathers, continued to lead me to greater places of freedom.

Chapter 3

Meeting Some Dads

Encountering the Father through spiritual fathers was foundational to my journey into freedom. These spiritual dads brought security; much needed identity and affirmation that filled the empty chasm of my heart. Embracing spiritual papas meant learning to release a multitude of fears that don't die easily—fear of being hurt, rejected and punished.

One thing I acquired growing up was the misleading ability to please people. I say misleading because no matter how well you master the art, it is not truly who you are. This charade keeps your true identity hidden. Early on I recognized the *ostracization* of those who step out, speak out, or live out their uniqueness. It could have been a result of seeing others being shunned or simply that I wanted to avoid criticism, but the end result was that I went overboard in my attempts to avoid the disapproval of others.

For me, serving God required being a fool in the eyes of the world, which was okay, as long as loved ones affirmed me. In the context of church life, much of the applause I craved came from being worshipful, bold with my public witness and spiritually devout—all admirable qualities. However, I didn't realize that my desire for God was fueled in part by my need for affirmation and affection from the ones I esteemed.

I am thankful that my Christian heritage included being raised in a pastor's home. But this also presented challenges. People often put you on a pedestal and I, although unknowingly, worked hard to stay there. I did not realize how unhealthy I was until I decided to step into an arena that did not generate applause from those who esteemed me.

I had never experienced a lack of affirmation from my spiritual leaders until I began to pursue the fresh outpouring of God's presence, which was outside the normal experience accepted in our church groups. To my surprise, I felt anger, disappointment and even wrath from many I had worked so long to please. I began to realize that this was God's incredibly kind and loving way of revealing just how unhealthy the foundation of my life had become and that He wanted me to break free. Living under the bondage of pleasing people, whether leaders or peers, had to be broken. This stronghold crippled my ability to be free and pursue the fullness of God's purposes in my life. Slowly but surely God began to free me from its hold.

Do I now blame people for rejecting me as I ventured into unchartered spiritual waters? No! Exploring new territory in God was truly about finding a healthy foundation based on God's validation... not man's.

In many church circles you are loved when you are in agreement, but written off when you think or act differently. This kind of conditional love is established on the fact you both agree on the same principles, ways of life and value system. God's love, however, is not based on this principle. As mentioned previously from Romans 5:8, *"But God demonstrates his own love for us in this: While we were still sinners, Christ died for us."* When we embrace this remarkable truth, it will bring us to a place of solid, unwavering confidence. Outside the culture of unconditional love and acceptance I discovered that differences are often met with sadness, disappointment, anger or even the silent treatment. God's love is not based on how perfect or imperfect our lives are. He loved us while we were still sinners! I began to experience this unconditional love through many different spiritual fathers. I wish I could share about every father who impacted my life, but due to time and space I can only mention a few.

One of the first to invest into me was Wes Crone. I first met this caring man when I encountered God at the family camp where my journey to freedom began. Although we lived several hours apart we kept in contact through frequent phone calls and occasional visits.

He became the voice of an affirming father in my life. Although I had received affirmation growing up, Wes provided a fresh touch of the Father's love. Our conversations touched various areas of my life and generally went something like this:

"Wes, I feel so terrible about myself. I don't like this area of my life...I'm not happy about what is going on in this situation...I feel terrible about these thoughts going on in my head."

"Keith, you are loved just as you are. God made you the way you are and He likes you. Don't be so hard on yourself. God's love is without condition, Keith, and you need to know how much He loves you."

I felt freedom to share personal struggles—struggles that, while common left me feeling terrible about myself; struggles relating to maintaining a heart and mind of purity. As I shared how badly I felt about myself, Wes modeled the Father's unconditional acceptance by sharing how proud he was of me. He stressed that God loved me and that I needed to accept myself as the Father accepted me and not allow shame to rob me of my identity as a son.

Kris Vallotton, another father who became a significant voice in my life, came on the scene when I had no framework within which to understand his gifting. Heather and I stayed at a friend's cabin deep in the Redwoods with Kris and a team of ministry students. While sharing a meal after returning from a meeting late one night, he spoke prophetically into our lives. We were not very familiar with the prophetic at that time, especially not from such a seasoned prophet. We were blown away by the specific things he shared with us, both from our history and present reality. He addressed leadership issues in our church revealing strategies the Lord wanted us to utilize. Kris also spoke about certain individuals to be wary of and areas of relationship growth we needed to pursue. He confirmed and revealed anointing and gifting in both Heather and myself, some of which we had yet to recognize. The level of accuracy with which Kris spoke into our lives was like receiving food in the midst of a famine.

That night we stayed up late writing down all we could recall of Kris's ministry to us, talking excitedly about this encounter. Later on someone prophesied over us that we would be mentored by Kris Vallotton out of a relationship that began in a cabin. They had no idea we had already experienced that encounter.

As time progressed, our lives frequently intersected with Kris. He spoke to us about many life-changing things. Because it required three and a half hours via car to reach Kris, Heather and I had much time to converse during our trips. I would plan out the various topics I wanted to address, none of which were ever discussed upon arrival. Sometimes on our way home, pain from the areas we dealt with in our conversations revealed the areas of much-needed growth in our lives. This was a level of fathering I had never experienced.

Our lives were quickly being transformed. It seemed as if every area was touched through spiritual parenting. It was freeing to find an outlet to talk about our marriage, finances, leadership skills, church, family parenting, future, past...you name it, we talked about it. It had been our dream to be mentored by people who carried the Father's heart. Kris spoke into our identities, affirming and confirming who we are and what we are called to do in this life. He provided wisdom in areas in which we needed counsel. He gave correction when needed, as well as encouragement. I am so thankful for his voice, friendship, loving care and wisdom.

Welcoming voices like Kris, Wes and so many others, brought me deeper into God's heart. It was a place of freedom where every part of me was intimately seen, yet still embraced and loved. Many times I would meet with one of them, fearing punishment or anger when I shared a struggle in our lives or our church, but each time my spiritual fathers met me with love and welcomed me with open arms. It seems like that would be an easy thing to receive, but it is uncanny how deeply entrenched the fear of rejection and punishment was in my belief system. Despite my struggles in this area, God faithfully removed layer after layer of rejection and the fear of man that had plagued me.

I am thrilled that there are "fathers" emerging all over the earth, both male and female, who embody aspects of the Father's heart. Fathers are utterly vital to the life flow of God released in and through us. I honestly know that without the many voices that carried The Father's heart in my life, I would not be here today authoring this book.

The Apostle Paul was an excellent example of the Father's love. He said in Romans 1:11, *"I long to see you so that I may impart to you some spiritual gift to make you strong…"* Paul wanted those entrusted to his care to succeed and experience God's best and highest in their lives. He not only shared great teaching and released needed power…he shared his life.

1 Corinthians 4:15-16 says, *Even though you have ten thousand guardians in Christ, you do not have many fathers, for in Christ Jesus I became your father through the gospel. Therefore I urge you to imitate me.*

Acquiring fathers in your life is crucial if you want to avoid reinventing the wheel in every area of your struggle. The men and women the Lord gave me not only shared wisdom, but also stories of their failures and successes. While it is true that many of my lessons were painful, it is also true that without the life experiences from each one, the learning curve would have greatly increased.

Fathers bring much needed identity into our lives. Once again we go back to a scripture used earlier and recall that before Jesus did one ounce of ministry the heavenly Father spoke from heaven in Matthew 3:17 saying, *"…This is my Son, whom I love; with him I am well pleased."* Fathers declare who we are apart from our performance. This sets us free from the approval of man and reinforces that God has already declared us to be significant, loved and pleasing to Him. Many times my mentors spoke over my identity declaring, "Keith, you are a teacher." "You have a prophetic voice." "You are a good son." "You are a loving pastor." "You have what it takes." These declarations, often spoken over me in times of inadequacy, caused me to rise to a higher level of identity. Words of identity from fathers release us from performance-oriented love into a place of security, knowing that we are already approved and pleasing to God.

There was a time when I was feeling extremely uptight about taking my prophetic gift to the next level. I was concerned if I did not continue to find outlets to use my gift it would be taken from me. One of the prophetic voices in my life spoke, "Keith, you need to relax. You have a prophetic gifting; it will function better out of rest then out of striving." After he spoke that over me I began to relax and stop striving to prophesy and my gift climbed to a much higher level. Fathers can impart identity in such a way that it brings much needed peace, rest and increased fruit in our lives.

Fathers also bring us into a place of security and safety, where fear diminishes. My frequent travels to other countries caused me to fret about my safety and the safety my family. During those times I felt the comforting effect of fatherly voices speaking peace and security.

One of my favorite prophetic fathers is Wendell McGowan. He embodies a Biblical Elijah fire while displaying grace and love, backed by boldness. Many times before a meeting, when I was feeling anxious about the tension and spiritual warfare in the atmosphere, I would phone him. His words of clarity and understanding regarding what was taking place in the spiritual realm helped salve my heart and revealed that good was coming my way. Other times I would feel afraid about my children's safety going into new spiritual territory and Wendell's prophetic insights combined with his understanding of the Father's goodness to protect His own, brought me back to a place of trusting peace.

There were times when I called upon Wendell because of something that had troubled the dreams of either my children or myself. I was still operating out of a fear-based mindset and he helped me recognize what God was doing and to discern what those dreams symbolized. Often, within dreams I viewed as being bad, he would find the heart of redemption, blessing and life. I left my conversations with Wendell feeling safe, secure and convinced that Jeremiah 29:11 was the Father's heart for me. *"For I know the plans I have for you,"* declares the Lord, *"plans to prosper you and not to harm you, plans to give you hope and a future."* Those who carry the Father's heart release the same heart to us, causing us to rest securely in the Father's embrace. After a while we find ourselves renewed inwardly, possessing the same mindsets as the earthly fathers who speak into us. We are free to trust that God is good and to understand He desires to protect what concerns us.

Fathers help bring us to a place of trusting God's plans for our lives while at the same time providing the serenity of knowing that we, and those we love, need not fear deception. Without spiritual dads we have difficulty staying on the right course in life and ultimately make many unnecessary blunders. When I lacked wisdom I knew I could call on one of my spiritual fathers who had walked the road before me. This brought tremendous peace and security to me as well as those under my care.

Fathers also bring needed correction in our lives. Many times Kris Vallotton, among others, saved me from unnecessary harm and pain by giving a word of correction. Sometimes as a young, zealous pastor I did not recognize that I was running rough shod over people in my passion to advance the Kingdom. Sometimes I did not know that I was in the middle of making unwise decisions, or treating people wrongly. Punishment terrified me, so God graciously gave me fathers to lovingly call me on my issues.

I had become extremely adept at putting up a polished, charismatic front that could fool others. Because I am gifted, love people and am fiercely passionate, I can come across healthier than I truly am. I thank God for Kris, who could see past my façade, see right to the issue with an eagle eye. Sometimes Heather and I would visit Kris for a spiritual check-up and he would ask me, "How are you doing?" I would remark, "Just fine." Kris would then turn to Heather and say, "How is Keith really doing?" She would bring out in the open the reality of our life. He knew how to get down to the heart of the matter even when I didn't.

Although I used this passage and analogy before it's worth repeating. Hebrews 12:5-6, in the Message Bible clearly conveys Biblical discipline. *My dear child, don't shrug off God's discipline, but don't be crushed by it either. It's the child he loves that he disciplines; the child he embraces, he also corrects. God is educating you; that's why you must never drop out. He's treating you as dear children. This trouble you're in isn't punishment; it's training, the normal experience of children.*

Punishment is rooted in fear, control, shame and other destructive characteristics whereas correction is discipline designed to help strengthen areas of weakness in our lives until we become mature in those areas.

Fathers bring many benefits. You may ask, "How do I find these kinds of relationships?" Before we can truly receive encouragement or discipline from the voices of fathers and mothers the Lord brings our way we first must learn to embrace and trust those whose views may differ from ours. If we are going to be ones who attract quality mentors it is essential that we learn to be gracious to those with whom we disagree. In the next chapter I want to share the experiences the Lord gave me as I learned to value such voices.

Chapter 4

The Secret Weapon of Value

Everyone enjoys a movie where the good guy rebels against systems of control, dishonesty and corruption. There is something in us that desires justice and freedom from wrong restraints. But, before you can be entrusted with the anointing that shakes up the status quo you must first learn how to honor those with whom you disagree. For me, learning to value those with whom I disagreed was key to becoming someone who could transform cultures.

I grew up in doctrinally similar churches my whole life. These churches established many necessary foundations of truth. The negative side of being surrounded by doctrinally similar people was that we primarily connected relationally because we agreed on the same teachings. This form of relationship developed the mindset that friends are people with whom I agree. If I were to ever explore a place I had never been spiritually or naturally, I would have to learn to appreciate input I did not understand. Additionally, I had no appreciation for spiritual activities that did not fit my framework of what approved spiritual activities must look like. For example, the acceptable spiritual activities in my church were speaking in tongues, an occasional public prophecy and fervent prayer. When I entered church settings where people laughed in the Spirit, soaked in God's presence, or fell under the power of an explosive anointing, I was repulsed. Anyone outside of my norm was just that...outside. They were not allowed to be an influence in my life because I did not agree with them.

How would I venture to places I had never been if I only hung around people with similar experiences as my own? I did not realize how my mindset actually created a resistance to the very thing for which my heart cried out. I wanted more of God. But more of God existed outside my present understanding, friendship circles and influencers. On one hand I was teachable, while on the other hand resistant to truth. I was teachable if I agreed with the teachings or way of conducting church. Was that true teachability when all I heard were things I already knew? Although I possessed a heart to learn and glean from my mentors, some of whom were considered cutting edge spiritual leaders for their time, each new level required new voices — voices that did not exist in my circle of influence. I was very skeptical of embracing anyone who was different from me.

My mindset told me that in the last days many would be deceived. How did I keep myself from being deceived? By never trusting anything or anyone I did not understand, or any experience I had not seen in the Bible. My view of how God could accomplish things was limited to the spiritual expressions that had become habitual in my life. There was so much more available than my norm but I was not about to venture into something foreign.

Even though I occasionally dared to disagree with the authority figures present in my life, I wasn't always honest in my disagreements. As a result, I found myself putting up a front and failing to reveal the hidden places inside of me that were in disagreement with their values or patterns of thinking. Courageous, truthful relationships with authority figures were a definite challenge for me. Let me share a few stories about how I experienced a breakthrough from these crippling mindsets.

The week before September 11, 2001, the Lord gave me the longest prophetic word I had received up to that point in my life. He told me I would go through a process of accusation and when I learned joy in the process, He would remove the accusation and increase the anointing. Yikes, what a bittersweet prophetic word! Anyone out there want that one? Amazingly, it brought peace to me about what lay ahead. A week later during the time of America's devastation from terrorist attacks, a group of leaders from my church required a change on my part. They said, "We are tired of what is happening in this church, Keith." In their words, "We want the old Keith back and we're giving you two weeks to find him. If you don't we are going to take as many people out of this church as possible." We even heard from members who still confided in us that these leaders were going so far as to encourage people to withhold finances so we would be forced to resign.

The leaders who asked me to return to a former Keith were friends of mine...some very close friends. The challenge was our disagreement. We did not yet have a culture that embraced diverse worship styles, emphasis in teaching, or different opinions. Our culture thrived on agreement. This is a positive attribute as long as you agree, but how do you reconcile disagreement in this case? My fellow leaders disagreed with me as much as I disagreed with them. At one time I stood against the type of spiritual culture I now nurtured in my life and others. God had radically changed me, and because of it, I became an avid defender of this fresh outpouring. I was slightly arrogant in how I advocated the new move of God. I possessed the mentality that went something like this: "Even if you do not understand where we are going, come along anyway. I am the boss and this is what we are doing." God was weeding this unhealthy approach out of my thoughts and actions.

I did not agree with, nor understand everything that was going on in this new move, but something in my spirit had changed for the better and I could not return to an old way of life. I had tasted of the new and would never stop partaking of it. I watched as friends, leaders and a few new converts were pulled out of the church. The leaders of our parent denominational organization received a long letter from these disgruntled congregants sharing the "heresies" of our church, my overbearing leadership style and a few other miscellaneous accusations. The leaders called me into several meetings and interrogated me about these reports. The week prior to this meeting, I had spoken at a sectional ministers gathering to report on the signs and wonders happening in our church, but now I was sitting there alone and on trial, assured by my denominational leaders that I was, indeed, in error.

At one particular church service, those from the congregation who opposed me, appeared and stood in watchful contemplation at the back of the room. As I entered, they ducked their heads in an attempt to avoid conversation, but I approached each one, gave them a hug and told them that I loved them. Later on, one of those who had been swept away in this season returned to our church because of the unconditional love I had demonstrated that day.

The denominational meetings continued as I was compelled to answer to higher and higher levels of leadership. These well-respected men who continually sided with the accusations brought against me had been my heroes. For a while I had a growing disagreement with their style of leadership, the lack of relationship in our network of churches, the need to wear suits and ties to every meeting (suits did not feel authentic to the region I pastored) and a number of other issues. As a result I entered these meetings with an arrogant attitude, rebelliously wearing khaki shorts and a Hawaiian shirt. I was disgruntled and had spoken to a few other pastors behind the scenes, but now I had my "day in court." When it came time for me to speak, I very clearly let my accusing leaders know that I was in complete disagreement with them; that they did not know what was happening in our church body, in our meetings and certainly did not recognize the move of God that was taking place. In spite of that, they still chose to believe the letter of accusation, a decision that absolutely crushed me! The ironic part of this whole thing is that these men who were now aligned solidly against me were the same men who only a few years earlier had empowered my efforts to shut down this new move of God. Because of their attitude, I turned against them having not yet learned how to honor authority figures with whom I disagreed.

Here is a principle worth remembering: Honor is not primarily evident when you agree, but rather, when you disagree. I did not honor my fellow leaders at this point and the result was growing tension. I arrogantly defied the protocol of dress and pushed this new move of God in every circle of ministry I stepped into, bringing the wrath of these leaders upon me. They required me to enter a disciplinary process wherein I provided monthly records of our church finances and weekly attendance. Each month I sent a report and each time I received a nasty letter, threatening to remove me from the group of churches if I did not adhere to their demands. If our church body dipped below a certain number of members they threatened to take over.

New friends in the move of God we now embraced were a source of strength and hope to us during this season. Our church shrank very quickly and before long we were a small group of people. My name was no longer honored in our denomination; I had become a black sheep in local and regional church circles. It was a very humbling time for me.

Despite the challenges I faced, God overhauled my heart, teaching me to honor leaders with whom I fiercely disagreed. My love for them was tested as I learned to respect their requests even though I disagreed with the values behind them. This process continued and just when I thought it was over...it extended another six months...and another six months...ultimately stretching out over a period of two years or so. By then we had lost so many members I felt like a complete failure and suggested to one of our elders that it may be time for me to resign. I had no vision; nothing left to offer our church body. Even though I felt that the church would be better off replacing me, that elder said, "Absolutely not, Keith!" We prayed and wrestled our way through my desire to quit.

The Lord came to me at this low point and said, "Keith, now I am going to build this church. When people ask you how you did it, you will say it was by my grace. It was not by a formula, but simply by the grace you received from me and from the fivefold ministry I sent your way to help." Shortly after this visitation things in our church body began to take a turn for the better.

Heather and I felt so much shame as a result of the grueling process we had been forced to endure that we attended few of our denominational minster's meetings. However, there was one meeting we really wanted to attend because of the special guest speaker. We made the decision to go and at one of the evening services we heard a message on returning to your first love. The speaker gave two altar calls. One altar call targeted those who had lost their first love. They needed to come to the altar and renew their vows with the Lord. Most of the ministers came up for this altar call. Heather and I did not, as we knew our love for the Lord was flourishing and we had been captured by His affection. The speaker gave another altar call inviting those who had been pursuing God to come forward. When he said that God wanted to give each person a special blessing, Heather and I couldn't get down there fast enough.

Keep in mind we were in a process of learning to honor those with whom we disagreed. We valued them and did not want to cause a ruckus. We were careful not to show any foreign emotion in worship or ministry that existed outside their levels of comfort. I had worn nice clothing that evening so as not to offend our leaders. Despite our efforts to conform honorably, God has a good sense of humor and unbeknownst to us — had an ace up His sleeve.

As we walked to the altar area the special speaker approached us. He never laid hands on us, but as he got near we were both knocked to the ground. I began to release a loud roar under the unction of the Spirit. I had never experienced this type of encounter. Noises and groaning came out of my belly from the Spirit of God, "Show...ho!" I cried loudly, which was not normal for these meetings and was certainly not intentional on my part. I lay right at the feet of the lead ministers who had handled my "heresy" case for two years. The accusations they dealt with covered this very area of Holy Spirit manifestations. Smack dab in front of my accusers the Lord increased the anointing with His manifest presence just like He had promised two years earlier, the week prior to September 11th. I learned to value my lead ministers and not purposefully disrespect them. More importantly, I learned to honor the Lord.

Heather and I gave the head of our church organization a small, but sincere sacrificial offering that night to illustrate the love and value we had for him. Shortly after this, we were called into one more meeting with the leadership overseeing our case. I wore a suit and tie. They ended the disciplinary process with me and our relationships were supernaturally restored. For several years following, they occasionally received a negative report by remaining disgruntled church body members. Those same leaders now quickly defended me to those whom brought accusation.

The reason I shared this story was to illustrate that I had to learn to value and appreciate those who did not change their way of thinking to accommodate mine. I learned to hear the heart of what others said to better understand what God was attempting to teach me. That did not mean I needed to agree with their direction, it simply meant that in this season, the Lord was teaching me how to value those different than me. Until I understood this, I would not be promoted. You may have a strong desire to reach your destiny, but to do so there is a process you must go through. Pastor friends would tell me, "Keith, you have every right to leave your denomination," but the Lord restrained me because His desire was to teach me how to value those with whom I disagreed.

Paul understood this in Acts 23:3-5, *Then Paul said to him, "God will strike you, you whitewashed wall! You sit there to judge me according to the law, yet you yourself violate the law by commanding that I be struck!" Those who were standing near Paul said, "You dare to insult God's high priest?" Paul replied, "Brothers, I did not realize that he was the high priest; for it is written: 'Do not speak evil about the ruler of your people.'*

When Paul realized whom he was talking to, he repented and changed his language. Though Paul continues to make his case he does it in an honorable way. In my experience, in order to get to where God wanted me to be in this fresh outpouring, I first had to learn how to respectfully disagree with those around me.

During this time, the Lord taught me that whether people were for or against me, I had to learn to value them if I wanted to gain the blessings available through them, or from the situation. Like a double-layered cake, honor has layers of its own. The foundational layer is a heart that values others. The second layer, the one most visible, is choosing the right language. If your language appears to value others but your heart does not truly honor them, you have hypocrisy. 1 Peter 2:17 states in the KJV, *"Honour all men. Love the brotherhood. Fear God. Honour the king."*

Every person is created in the image of God and, therefore, each is valuable and worthy of being honored. Nobody is trash. It does not matter how wrong you think someone might be in terms of theology, beliefs or whether they are steeped in sin and wickedness. People are valuable.

Heather and I visited a particular gallery to view the art of our friend, Deborah Crone. As we looked through the gallery I noticed some small paintings by an artist we were unfamiliar with. Some of his works were priced at $30,000-$40,000. When I inquired as to why they were so expensive, I was informed that the artist used to paint pictures of nobility in England and several of his paintings now hung in Buckingham Palace. Because royalty had purchased some of his art, the value of all his paintings skyrocketed.

As wonderful and valuable as those paintings are, we are even more valuable as sons and daughters of the King, made in His image. The master painter painted us, and then declared, "You are incredibly valuable. So valuable, the price I am going to pay to purchase you, my prized possession, is the lifeblood of My son, Jesus." This means that not only did God purchase us with Jesus' blood; He bought us while we were still sinners. We, in turn, do not value people because they are perfect or agreeable but because the Creator bestowed value on them; because they are made in the image of the greatest King even if they have not yet yielded to His Kingship. Matthew 5:43-44 says, *"You have heard that it was said, 'Love your neighbor and hate your enemy.' But I tell you, love your enemies and pray for those who persecute you."*

Many people state, "I will show love and respect them when *they* respect me." I used to feel that way myself. Once I was complaining to Kris Vallotton that some of the people in my church did not honor me as a leader. He said, "Keith, you cannot expect them to honor you first as a leader. You have to model honor toward them by honoring them when they do not honor you. You have to teach them to honor by honoring." Not exactly my first inclination when feeling the pain of dishonor, but it is what great leaders do. They do not live their lives as victims of their circumstance. Great leaders *change* circumstances, creating the atmosphere they wish to live in.

1 Peter 2:17 exhorts the believer to, *"Honor the King."* It's important to note that the "King" Peter references was evil king Nero, who, at that very time, was killing and torturing many believers. He was feared and hated, a harsh man unworthy of respect. The scripture, however, makes it clear that we are to honor those in authority, no matter their heart condition. Many people honor those with whom they agree, with whom they feel safe – and that is good. But sadly, they limit the blessing God has for them by not extending this principle of honor to those with whom they disagree or judge to be dishonorable.

Ephesians 6:2-3 says, *"Honor your father and mother (which is the first commandment with a promise) that it may be well with you, and that you may enjoy long life on the earth."* When the Lord told us to honor parents, leaders and those in authority it was not conditional on their actions being honorable or respectable. This does not mean we have to obey everything they tell us to do, but it does mean we respectfully treat them as a valuable painting in God's art gallery of creation. Honor is quite often the means by which God will draw people to the message of the cross.

The prophet Daniel understood this Kingdom principle. Even though king Nebuchadnezzar was directly responsible for Daniel and the entire nation of Israel being held in Babylonian captivity, after interpreting the king's dream, Daniel responded honorably, saying, "My lord, if only the dream applied to your enemies and its meaning to your adversaries!" (Daniel 4:19) In other words, the correction revealed through the interpretation of the dream was not something Daniel desired to see come upon the King. That is the true heart of a person who honors another. According to Kingdom principles, whether a person is or is not walking with God is inconsequential. They are still worthy of honor. God honored Daniel with promotion because Daniel honored the king, evil though he was.

We must not mistake honor for agreement. When we honor a person we learn how to value them, see the gold inside and draw it out. The one person we are ultimately called to obey is King Jesus. Once again we look at 1 Peter 2:17. Notice it says, *"Honour all men. Love the brotherhood. Fear God. Honour the king."* We are called to honor and value everyone, but the one we are to fear is God. Notice that it doesn't say to be "afraid" of God, but to fear Him, i.e. to revere Him. He is the one whose approval we live from.

David, king of Israel, is a great example of this. Every time he made a mistake — and he made some pretty hideous ones — grief over his sin sent him back to his knees. It is for this reason God referred to him as a "man after My own heart." This even after murdering one from his inner circle and committing adultery with the man's wife. What set David apart from all others of his day was the fact that he "feared" the Lord and those who fear God will experience His blessing. At the end of the day, it is God we seek to please. Even if people are displeased with you...if God is pleased with you, then it is a good day.

God has also placed people in our lives who we have to learn to respect and obey, at times submitting even when we do not want to. If we are to be entrusted with the anointing required to start a reformation, we must be teachable and moldable. We cannot embrace the "Lone Ranger" method of leadership. Paul the Apostle learned how to be sent, instead of simply venturing out on his own. He spent several years in preparation before being sent out from his local church.

Acts 13:1-2, *In the church at Antioch there were prophets and teachers: Barnabas, Simeon called Niger, Lucius of Cyrene, Manaen (who had been brought up with Herod the tetrarch) and Saul. While they were worshiping the Lord and fasting, the Holy Spirit said, "Set apart for me Barnabas and Saul for the work to which I have called them."*

Trusting that God will never put us in a place that is going to destroy us is key to valuing those who are in a place of authority in our lives. The spiritual landscape is littered with those who have attempted to take the world while trampling on relational boundaries in their home, work and church. They assume that their "calling" gives them permission to leave a scorched earth in their wake. Before you can be trusted with the revolutionary anointing of Jesus, the disciples, or anyone in the Bible who sought His Kingdom, you must first understand how to function in relationships that are not perfectly cohesive.

In the next chapter I will discuss how to identify when it's time to throw off constraint and move into the place where God has called you even though it's not received in your present circles.

Chapter 5

Starting a Revolution

As you progress in your walk toward greater freedom there may come a time when you must throw off the restraints of your present situation. As I progressed in my journey with God I realized that my personal belief system and those of my present church organization were in conflict. These views did not concern salvation through Jesus Christ, the Godhead or other foundational doctrinal beliefs. They had to do with the manifestation of the Holy Spirit in public meetings, the disapproval of present relationships and whether or not prophets and apostles exist today. The church organization of my childhood had provided me with a rich heritage that I dearly love, but now operated under an entirely different set of standards — standards I no longer embraced.

One of the challenges had to do with the reality that our presiding officials were only present when a complaint, problem, or disciplinary action arose. These voices were not present in our lives as caring fathers, but rather, as corporate administrators. I felt like I was just another pastor who could easily be discarded if disagreement prevailed. I began to draw closer and closer to an emerging circle of new fathers in my life. These men made personal visits on a regular basis, along with a steady stream of phone calls and emails in an intentional effort to communicate love and nurture. Heather and I were embraced by a completely new group of people who knew and valued us as unique individuals.

A chain of events several years later set off the absolute severance between our church denomination and us. Our local church body had been under this organization's covering for many years before I pastored there. At one point we realized we could no longer stay in what we perceived to be an inflexible wineskin. Those who simply tolerated us had to be left behind as we moved forward into a place where we were celebrated. In order for this to happen, our church had to step out from under the covering and licensing provided by our present denomination. We longed for a place where our covering aligned with the new, astonishing territory that God was revealing to us. The grace to continue in the old framework had lifted and we heard God calling us to move on.

When our leadership finally made the decision to leave the land of our roots we did not receive a parting blessing. Even one of my grandfathers chose not to bless me as I requested. These were his roots as well and he informed me I needed to stay with the "tried and true." This was excruciatingly painful for me. I valued my Grandpa's affirmation and it was one of the few times he did not extend it. A few months later he passed on to be with the Lord. I am incredibly thankful for the legacy he left me and although he did not agree with my direction in this present situation, he did bless us before he died.

The leaders presiding over our church organization wrote letters of accusation and warned us that if we left we would be placed on the "black list," which meant we wouldn't be able to minister at any churches under their covering. Despite this we knew we must continue on with what we felt in our heart.

Fear of being punished by those we had walked with for so long was outweighed by our excitement over what lay ahead. Although we were anxious to get moving, having already navigated our way through a two-year preparation process, we wanted to allow our church time to process this decision. They needed to be persuaded in their own hearts that this direction was from God. Each board member decided in his heart it was God and we presented the decision to our church members for a vote. A week before this process was completed I had the revelation that for the first time in my life I could make decisions without fear of repercussions. During the first years of learning to move with God in this new venture I knew that every time I made a decision, attempted something new, or embraced new manifestations of His power and presence there would be a backlash. The thought of actually being free of this bondage was simply wonderful.

We did not leave without first seeking the counsel of fathers who could speak into us personally and corporately on a regular basis — fathers who truly knew and celebrated us. Our covering had gone from corporate to relational.

If you want to harvest the fruit of what God has called you to see, there may come a time when you have to throw off the restraints of your leadership covering. Many people remain in a particular church, or under the same leadership out of a sense of loyalty. Loyalty is not honor. Loyalty means you refuse to leave, no matter how wrong that person is. Honor means you can be courteous and still value each leader as a person while at the same time disagreeing theologically, even to the point of parting ways. I had learned to honor those going in a different direction, but the Lord no longer required me to be loyal to these leaders. He asked me to be loyal to Him.

At first I had assumed it was my job to turn around the ship that was our church organization, but the Lord was not interested in that at the moment. He was interested in me leaving a relationship of tolerance and coming into what He was doing for us in the Spirit. The late East German dissident Rudolph Bahro said, "When the forms of an old culture are dying, the new culture is created by a few people who are not afraid to be insecure." You cannot throw off restraints until you learn to honor those who restrain you. It is crucial to carefully choose your words and the timing of those words when you disagree.

In the same way a chick struggles against the eggshell at birth, restraints often remain in place for a season for the purpose of providing resistance against which we wrestle, in order to build the strength necessary to ultimately cast them off. If the egg is cracked too soon, the chick will die because its strength is not fully developed. The same principle applies when we begin to recognize that God has more for us. As we learn to honorably disagree, our resolve for the *more* of God grows and grows.

Isaiah 10:27 says, *"In that day their burden will be lifted from your shoulders, their yoke from your neck; the yoke will be broken because you have grown so fat."* The word "fat" in this verse means anointing. The anointing will break the yoke as you continue to grow in the revelation of Christ within you and His plan for your freedom. Eventually the anointing becomes so full in you it will break your present restraints. Restraints put on you by man, leaders and even yourself; restraints holding you back from the freedom God created each one of us to walk in and enjoy.

We are in the middle of a major reformation. The church cannot stay the same. Status quo will never get us where we are called to go in the Kingdom. We must break free of the "predictable" in which we have become comfortable. I am not interested in being cantankerous or angry at an organization. I am interested in bringing the fullness of His Kingdom to earth. He has called us to make the Kingdoms of the world, the Kingdom of our God—and this requires a revolution. We will not arrive there with many of the present wineskins of today's church organizations. A few of the apostles understood this well.

In Acts 4, Peter and John had just healed a man who could not walk. This healing, along with their message of the resurrection of the dead, greatly disturbed the Jewish church leaders. They threatened Peter and John, ordering them not to speak in the name of Jesus. *But Peter and John replied, "Judge for yourselves whether it is right in God's sight to obey you rather than God. For we cannot help speaking about what we have seen and heard."* (Acts 4:19-20) As the story unfolds, persecution continues to grow. In Acts 5 they are again warned about preaching in Jesus' name, then severely beaten. Despite the warning and punishment they continue to spread their message.

Many moves of God persist even though the fathers of the previous move reject the fathers of the fresh move. It is sad to say, but many times the fathers of previous moves of God are the very ones who persecute the emerging fathers. Why do fresh moves of God exist? Because wineskins become inflexible and inflexible wineskins ultimately stifle life. Leaders who have ceased to be true fathers and have become merely administrators of organizations often resort to maintaining the machine of religion through intimidation and control.

We all know the story of Moses. He was born at a time when the Egyptians oppressed the Israelites. As a baby, Moses was rescued from death by an Egyptian Princess and raised in a royal household. Later, in a misguided effort to defend his fellow Israelites, Moses killed one of the Egyptian oppressors. This action angered the ruling Pharaoh and Moses fled the country. After forty years, God sent Moses back to Egypt. Exodus 8:1, *Then the Lord said to Moses, "Go to Pharaoh and say to him, 'This is what the Lord says: Let my people go, so that they may worship me."* The Lord does not want his people to be controlled or oppressed by anyone. He created every human being to be free.

Too often church structures that began with outpourings of freedom in the Spirit end up being prisons of control and the "taskmasters of tradition" set a watchful guard over programs that no longer hold life. As in *The Matrix* movie, people become nothing more than "batteries" used to keeping a system going. God is looking for living, loving relationships that overflow with freedom and joy, environments where dreams can be pursued and fulfilled. But it takes people of courage to create this kind of culture.

There is a right way and a wrong way to go forward and sadly, many people leave a church or close relationship in an unhealthy manner. They are discouraged by unmet expectations, or frustrated in their pursuit of the *more* of God. Oftentimes they lack the knowledge to depart in a way that honors their present leaders and the courage to work through relational disputes. As their disagreements and frustrations grow, they pull away from those with whom they fellowship. As their hearts grow cold toward their leaders, they care less about the relationship and more about nurturing the mounting bitterness in their hearts.

When bitterness is given free reign, the motivation often swings from caring about preserving honor to simply getting out of the offending relationship as quickly as possible. As a result, the church is often ripped to shreds by the harsh criticisms spoken toward church leaders and even friends. "God told me to leave." "God told me that this church couldn't be blessed." "The Lord said I needed to go to this other church." The end result of this type of relational dysfunction is that you wind up being no better than the ones supposedly holding you back.

When our church tasted the fresh expression of God's presence in our lives, as I shared in earlier chapters, we lost relationships. I noticed that those who had a root of bitterness, frustration and offense were the ones who got caught up into splitting and tearing apart the church. Unresolved frustration will not cause a revolution that brings life; rather it will cause a short-lived upheaval that brings destruction.

Matthew 18:34 *"In anger his master turned him over to the jailers to be tortured, until he should pay back all he owed."* Even if you feel genuinely hurt or mistreated, when you do not forgive and release others you invite torment into your life from the demonic realm. Unforgiveness or bitterness never ends well. Remember that how you start is most likely how you will end. God had called us to move out in pursuit of the *more* and we knew that our present wineskin could not take us there. But thankfully, we did not leave the land of our forefathers in bitterness. We had worked through disagreement and had learned to honor and value those who did not approve of our path.

Why is it that the way in which you leave restricted circumstances and the way in which you start a revolution is so important? It is because anything of lasting value must have a proper foundation. If I want to build a high rise I must first set a strong, unshakable foundation. If I do not set the foundations accurately I will have the Leaning Tower of Pisa on my hands. This is true in all areas of life.

If you leave a church, organization or community in bitterness, you risk becoming a lonely person full of discord, unable to find satisfying relationships. So many people wander from church to church, relationship-to-relationship, never content, always blaming everyone around them. The cycle never ends. They fail to notice the common denominator in each one of these churches or relationships is not the ever-changing people they encounter, but, rather, themselves.

One of the couples that left our church came from another situation where they had been discontented. They left our church with a group of people and ended up in yet another church for a short time, before finally leaving *that* church to find *another* church. To my knowledge, they have yet to find a suitable place to worship. As a pastor I have learned that if someone comes to me because they are displeased with their previous situation and want to partner with me, they will eventually become disillusioned and repeat the cycle. It does not matter how many times you feel the Lord has told you to leave; you need to get relationships right before you go anywhere. I encourage anyone feeling a call to the *more* of God to seek healing for underlying wounds and understanding for unmet expectations. You may find the place you desire to leave is, in fact, the place you need to plant yourself.

As a church leader I always wondered if I could handle being under another person's leadership. I enjoyed the freedom I felt as a pastor. Although I had many great fathers speaking into my life I knew that ultimately the decisions rested with me.

For a moment, allow me to jump ahead to a later season when we joined the staff of The Mission in Vacaville, California. When we moved to Vacaville we were excited to be a part of the dream and mission this church had created. These selfless people had paid a high price for what had become dear to our hearts. As I became established in this new city and church, what had once seemed so perfect, was slowly giving way to frustration. "If I was leading, I would do that differently." Uh-oh.

As time went on I found that I could not attend church services without being dissatisfied over how the service transpired. As a result, I began to distance myself emotionally from the ones with whom I used to share excitement. I wrestled with the expectations I brought with me. I had to let go of my notions of what a church service should look like. I had to realize my way of life, my approach, was not the only way and that there were other valid expressions of the Kingdom that were different than mine. I remember one Sunday finally coming to a place of resolve. "Lord, I accept this place as You created it to be." I felt peace flood in and was able to rejoice in the goodness of God and the way He was manifested through these dear believers. It was not an easy transition, but exceedingly worth it.

As my influence grew I realized that I could not operate with a victim mentality, hoping that someone would create the culture I enjoyed. Instead, I vowed to steward the venues entrusted to me and to intentionally pursue relationships. I understood that I did not have to wait for the fire of God—I could release the fire to create an encounter, partnering with the Holy Spirit to bring the Kingdom of God. I had thrown off the restraints of bitterness and feelings of insignificance... this was my time!

Some people stay on a dead horse long after it has died hoping to bring it back to life. "Well, it's not exactly dead. I want to bring revival to this place. I feel called to help the leadership experience the *more* of God." Take my word for it...as well intentioned as you might be, if the horse is "dead," dismount and bury the poor thing! I assumed I could change my denomination, but God had other plans. He wanted to change *me* and to send me where people hungered for what I carried; where people celebrated me; where my gifting and anointing were better suited to serve the body of Christ.

You can spend a lifetime of frustration trying to change those who do not desire change. Why not find friends you can enjoy and not simply tolerate? Why not determine to be a proactive part of your destiny instead of a victim of your circumstances? Instead of being a spiritual nomad, moving from place to place, invest the time to discover the root of your frustration. Only then will you be able to foster enduring relationships. Instead of adding bricks to your walls of rejection, face your fears and find acceptance in the arms of God and in loving relationships.

Perhaps you have been settled in a church for many years and have grown comfortable in long-term relationships...perhaps even healthy, fruitful relationships. Yet, something deep within your heart knows there must be more. I don't know about you, but I don't want a nice predictable life or nice predictable church meetings! I don't want a nice predictable God. I want more! I want the God of Elijah to be my God. I want the God who answers by fire to be the fire in me. I want to have a fire in my bones again. I know there are more adventures and I will find a group of people waiting to explore them with me.

It's time to fan into flame the coals of your heart that have grown cold. You are meant for the *more*. You are meant to see the fullness of His Kingdom come to earth. You are meant to see the fullness of His purposes come alive in your heart. You are meant to be a part of a revolution of people with violent love advancing the Kingdom of God. Matthew 11:12 says, *"From the days of John the Baptist until now, the kingdom of heaven has been forcefully advancing, and forceful men lay hold of it."*

The Kingdom of God does not advance through nice, tame Christianity. The Kingdom of God advances through people so full of the fire, of God's loving passion, they will not be silent anymore. They must spread the good news of the finished work of Jesus to the entire earth. God looks for a people who will advance His Kingdom at any cost. You are not called to be a part of a nice church, with nice programs and nice people. God is not nice! God is kind and gentle, but He is also a conquering warrior with eyes of fire, a sword coming out of His mouth and a rod of iron to rule the nations. As C.S. Lewis said, "He is not a tame lion!"

If you say yes to Him, you will join David who cut the head off of the giant of fear. If you say yes to Him you will join Daniel who was rescued from a den of lions. If you say yes to Him you will join Paul and Silas who were delivered from their chains as they sang God's praise. If you say yes to Him you will join Jesus who was accosted by demons, mobbed by crowds, crucified by the religious leaders and yet conquered death, hell and the grave.

Are you ready to be a part of a revolution, or will you continue to live in bitterness and frustration over your circumstances? Are you going to continually complain about the ever-increasing darkness on the earth, the evils of the day, the wickedness on television, the bleakness of our world's economy? Or are you going to join the army of Hebrews 11... people of overcoming faith who confronted Kings, witnessed the fall of evil empires, caused demons to flee, raised the dead, shut the mouths of lions and were joyfully martyred for what they believed?

You were meant for Kingdom revolution. I am not referring to waving protest signs in front of government buildings or standing on street corners shouting, "You are wrong, sinners, headed for hell." I am not referring to disgruntled, embittered, angry, cantankerous living. I am referring to being a part of God's army of joyfully intoxicated people, so overwhelmed by His love they cannot help but leak everywhere they go. I am referring to a band of brothers and sisters who do not battle with the weapons of this world, but love violently through acts of kindness, raw power, bold declarations and righteous pure living. I am calling you out of the chains of religion to be a part of an army of freedom fighters — fighters who will take the good news to all the earth. Will you be a part of this army?

Years ago my friends from Vacaville called me into this move of God telling me, "Keith, you were meant for this revival." And it's true! I am meant for this move of God...and so are you. I told the Lord I wanted to be a pioneer on the frontlines forging the way to see the fullness of heaven restored on earth and not just reading about it. I am not waiting for Jesus to return to whisk us out of this sin-torn, war-ravaged world. I am called to give Him the reward for His suffering. I am not here to allow darkness to spread, but to let my light so shine that it overwhelms the shadows over our land.

Many fear that in the end times things will become tremendously difficult and the enemy will prevail. That is not truth. Numerous places in the Old and New Testament encourage us that in the last days His Kingdom will come forth and rule. Isaiah 2:2-4 says, *In the last days the mountain of the Lord's temple will be established as chief among the mountains; it will be raised above the hills, and all nations will stream to it. Many peoples will come and say, "Come, let us go up to the mountain of the Lord, to the house of the God of Jacob. He will teach us his ways, so that we may walk in his paths." The law will go out from Zion, the word of the Lord from Jerusalem. He will judge between the nations and will settle disputes for many peoples. They will beat their swords into plowshares and their spears into pruning hooks. Nation will not take up sword against nation, nor will they train for war anymore.*

I believe that we are now in the last days and it is time for the army of the Lord to arise. The nations will come to the mountain of the Lord and we make up that mountain. Because the Lord is with us and *in* us, we have the answers to what the world is searching for, but they will never come to us if we espouse a defeated, end time eschatology. We must transform our thinking and rise up as the victorious bride of Christ.

In the last days God's Kingdom will rise up and never be conquered. Many people look at end time scriptures and view them through lenses of fear — fear that the world will cave in on them. I see in almost every chapter in the book of Revelation that the church overcomes, the enemy is defeated, Christ rules, the church rises up in heavenly places and brings heaven to earth. I see the nations coming into our walls and having healing released to them from the river of life flowing out of us. It is time for the people of God to embrace the revolution Jesus began over two thousand years ago. It is time we say yes to the mandate God gave to mankind at the beginning of time. Genesis 1:28, God blessed them and said to them, *'be fruitful and increase in number; fill the earth and subdue it. Rule over the fish in the seas and the birds of the air and over every living creature that moves on the ground.*

This is your calling and mine. He does not give us an assignment we cannot fulfill. You were born at the perfect time in history. This is your hour! Your time! Instead of continuing to hide behind fear while watching the enemy trample on the land God has given you as an inheritance, rise up! Throw off all restraints and begin to rule and reign with the King of Kings.

In order to be a revolutionary who pursues heartfelt dreams, blazing the trail to destiny, you must learn to recognize and embrace the spiritual fathers and mothers sent to help. In the next chapter I would like to discuss how the Lord taught me to pull these needed voices into my life — voices that guided me toward increase, health and longevity.

Chapter 6

Becoming a Bull's Eye for Blessing

A major key God used to accelerate me toward my destiny was learning how to welcome input from spiritual fathers and mothers. In the previous chapter, I discussed how and when to throw off restraints. But in order for this to happen successfully, you need to have spiritual mentors helping you make good decisions in these unchartered waters. In this chapter I will address how I learned to paint a target on my heart that attracted guidance. This ability to receive wisdom and have it saturate every area of life requires a high level of trust in both God and people — an ability that I had yet to develop.

I truly desired spiritual voices in my life, but receiving from them meant that I often had to trust a perspective I did not yet understand. This was challenging given my belief that in the last days people would be deceived — even the very "elect" — and I certainly didn't want to be one of those. As a result, I found myself continually on guard and very cautious about whom I trusted. At the time, I did not realize that my attitude would actually hinder opportunities for people to speak into my life. Surmounting the brick wall of fear I had constructed around my life required prophetic courage from my spiritual fathers and mothers. Thankfully, God had placed key people in my life who could do just that.

Another hurdle people had to overcome in order to reach me, was the level of control in which I operated. The message I communicated through my wrong attitude was, "Bless me...if you can." This attitude came from a fear of anything that existed beyond my scope. "What if I am being deceived?" "Was this God or man?" I stepped gingerly into these new, uncharted waters one inch at a time. I am so thankful that the Father in His tender mercy brought people into my life that could see through my fears, speak to the destiny inside of me and call it out.

An essential ingredient needed to attract the input of spiritual fathers is teachability. Being teachable means you are also moldable, and moldable people attract key voices. As mentioned previously, my resistance was largely due to fear of the unknown, but just as critical was a resistance that grew out of negative experiences with former spiritual fathers. This produced a stubborn guardedness resulting in me being unmoldable. Here's something I learned through this process: If you are perceived as being unteachable and unmoldable, people will not waste precious time banging their heads against the brick wall of your resistant heart. They will, instead, search for those who are pliable.

Kris Vallotton mentioned to me once that childcare would help our services tremendously, providing a much needed respite for people not blessed with a high tolerance for loud and rambunctious children in a church setting. To be honest, I didn't get it. I mean I was a parent and I had learned to ignore the noises and distractions that accompany young children, why couldn't everyone else? Heather and I attended a church service with Kris and brought our children along with us. Although I knew Kris's thoughts regarding childcare, instead of leaving our kids in the nursery, I chose to keep them with us — up front, near Kris where they made quite a lot of noise the whole time. When he approached me afterward and asked if I would please put them in the nursery, I flippantly replied, "Oh that's just you, Kris. It doesn't bother anyone else." He didn't say anything at that time...but a few months later during one of our "checkups," he addressed it.

We had a great meeting and at the end Kris remarked, "Hey Keith, you remember a few months ago when the situation happened with your children and you said, 'Oh that's just Kris,' and went on doing what you wanted anyway? That was dishonoring to me and I know that's not your heart." I valued Kris as a spiritual father and because of our relationship I was immediately convicted. Because I still struggled with an unteachable spirit, I had dishonored and hurt the very one who was desperately trying to help me. He wasn't being unkind or even especially demanding; he just had a greater understanding of the situation. He knew that uncontrolled children in church services could be a tipping point to new members staying or moving on.

In the end, far more important than this specific childcare issue was the manner in which I handled Kris's input and exposed my continuing lack of trust in spiritual fathers. His intention was not to target my disobedience, but, rather, the dishonor I had shown him. If you continually dishonor key spiritual fathers, it will cause them to withhold their wealth of knowledge. Spiritual fathers search for good soil in which to plant seeds of wisdom and if you are not ready for the seedling, then they will move on to someone who is. By missing out on fatherly wisdom, you will be prone to make mistakes that could have been avoided had you maintained an open heart. Proverbs 9:7-8 says, *Whoever corrects a mocker invites insults; whoever rebukes the wicked incurs abuse. Do not rebuke a mocker or he will hate you; rebuke a wise man and he will love you.*

The Lord continued to reinforce this truth by helping me understand that the reason people have resistant hearts is because they have been hurt. If the lens through which you view life is one of woundedness, it will produce a lack of trust in God's goodness that will keep you from blessing.

For three years I was in a relationship with an amazingly gifted and talented individual. While they could have benefited greatly from our interaction, their mistrust of me personally and leaders in general caused them to continually reject and question my motives. This prevented them from obtaining much needed momentum to advance the ministries God had given them. After three years I was quite frustrated and disheartened by the constant rejection, suspicion and fears they had about me. The Lord told me, "Keith, you can't work with mockers. They will constantly reject you and you will go away hurting. You can love them, but you will only get momentum with people who know they are loved, and from that place of love can trust."

It seems like trust issues always surface when we enter new territory. One time we had taken a ministry team to another country to conduct a prayer walk. As the walk progressed different people began accusing me of being harsh, demanding and forceful. It seemed like everything I asked of them was blown out of proportion. Finally, I had to gently say, "I know my actions may make you feel like you are being forced and that what I ask of you may remind you of a time when that was true, but you have to trust that my motives are right. I am not like your earthly father." In order for these individuals to move on, they had to make the choice to believe that what I said was true and choose to stop viewing me through the lens of mistrust. People who do not trust spiritual leaders because of past hurts will find themselves constantly hurt by leaders and instead of acceleration in their lives, they will wind up circling the "trust mountain" time and time again.

I know this to be true because I experienced this same struggle for many years. Throughout each meeting with Kris there was a constant loop running around in my mind: *I am going to get hurt. Something is wrong with me. I'm sure I will be punished.* Every time Kris tried to speak wisdom and truth into me, I left hurting. The end result was that even though our meetings were life changing and amazingly beneficial, I dreaded going.

After several years of operating out of this place of fear, my relationship with Kris was in danger of being ruined. One day he said, "Keith, I don't like to see you so hurt from our meetings. Maybe you need to find another mentor; one who you are better able to receive from." Even though I was thankful for the many voices the Lord had given me, I knew that if I lost Kris I would lose something very valuable, for his insight broke through my walls and dealt with my issues...issues that others saw but would not breach. I found myself at a crossroads facing a tough decision: Would I trust, or would I continue to hurt? I knew I had to climb higher so I said, "Kris, I need you in my life. This is not your issue, but mine. I want to grow in trust."

The day after I returned from this meeting, the Lord said, "The reason why you hurt so much, Keith, is that you have not learned to trust Me. You do not know that I am good and that I have brought Kris in your life to help raise you up. Trust Me, Keith and things will change."

I decided to trust.

The next time Kris offered advice I did not understand, I chose to go with it without question...advice, by the way, that proved to be very helpful. When I learned to trust Kris's insights—learned that his intentions were for my good—the pain of those meetings vanished. However, my lack of trust in other people seemed to diminish very slowly, and flushing out the depth of this revelation took a long time.

A great spiritual father and friend, Dave Crone, said something like this: "If you are afraid of a person, you can't minister together. Your fear of that person will cause you to sabotage what God would like to release." You cannot truly grow in a relationship in which you are afraid. You will constantly find yourself trying to please the other person, instead of the Lord, which is a hindrance to increase. Proverbs 29:25 says, *"Fear of man will prove to be a snare, but whoever trusts in the Lord is kept safe."* As you can see, in order to be teachable you have to trust and teachability is the key to attracting the blessings of wisdom into your life.

Another essential element required to attract blessing and insight into your life is humility. James 4:6 says, *"God opposes the proud but gives grace to the humble."* Pride is a know-it-all which boasts, "I am self-sufficient and in need of no other. I have gotten where I am today because of me." The prideful person does not recognize that it is grace that has enabled him to reach this place in life.

Titus 2:1 says, *"You must teach what is in accord with sound doctrine. Teach the older men..."* A few verses later in verse 11 and 12 Paul says, *For the grace of God has appeared that offers salvation to all people. It teaches us to say "No" to ungodliness and worldly passions, and to live self-controlled, upright and godly lives in this present age.* Paul is telling Titus he must teach what is appropriate. A few verses later Paul says that this grace, released through people, has the power to accomplish what we could not accomplish on our own. In order to receive this grace we must humble ourselves.

Once in a meeting the Lord revealed to me that a man who I had only just met had something I needed and that I would have to "duck low" to receive it. This man came from a different part of the country with a unique accent and different way of dress. For some reason I found his mannerisms to be off-putting and as a result, developed a resistance to receiving anything from him. But, the Lord had asked me to humble myself and push past those exterior things in order to receive the help he could provide...so, I ducked low.

I approached the man, asking him if he would pray for me and speak into my life anything he felt the Lord wanted me to receive. He prayed over me and presented a nugget of truth that was very helpful in an area of my struggle with trust. The humility required to look beyond his exterior and receive the wealth of spiritual inheritance in him provided a key that I may have had to search many years to find. If you want to receive the grace God has for you, you must first place yourself in a posture of humility. Only then will you be able to understand with whom God wants to enhance your life.

I have become relentless in the search for inheritance that the Lord has stored up for me along life's path. I find wisdom in believers, unbelievers, men, woman, children, the elderly, peers, fathers and mothers. I find wisdom in people, through books, CDs, television and more. I am always on the alert. Whenever I set foot in a meeting where I know there are potential gold mines available for excavation, I pay heed to those from whom I can receive, with whom I can enjoy friendship and those to whom the Lord would have me minister. All three of these components are not always present at the same time, but when I posture myself in this way I become a magnet for blessings, prophetic encouragement, wisdom, friendships, connections and open doors. This is not arrogance, but something I know I need for life, blessing, health and longevity. I do not sit, anxiously praying, "God if it be Your will, You will bring someone along." Rather, I actively search for His blessings.

Ephesians 6:1-3 says, *"Children, obey your parents in the Lord for this is right. Honor your father and mother- which is the first commandment with a promise- that it may go well with you and that you may enjoy long life on the earth."*

The key to long life is the honor we give to and the value we place *in* others. Earnestly seek the treasure God has deposited in His people. If you do, you will find acceleration in the processes of your life and may ultimately avoid challenges that others have had to face. One nugget of wisdom fully received will carry you on to greater heights.

Solomon was unique, not just because he received a download of wisdom from God, but also because he learned to receive wisdom from his father. Proverbs 4:3-9 says, *"When I was a boy in my father's house, still tender, and an only child of my mother, he taught me and said, 'Lay hold of my words with all your heart; keep my commands and you will live. Get wisdom, get understanding; do not forget my words or swerve from them. Do not forsake wisdom, and she will protect you; love her, and she will watch over you. Wisdom is supreme; therefore get wisdom. Though it cost all you have, get understanding. Esteem her, and she will exalt you; embrace her, and she will honor you. She will set a garland of grace on your head and present you with a crown of splendor.'"* And that is merely the groundwork of what Solomon learned from his parents. By collecting wisdom from his father, David, he was prepared to receive all of what God had to give to the point that he became the wisest man to ever live.

Do you want to be wise? Do you want to live a life of accelerated blessing? Then acquire wisdom, adopt a teachable posture and learn to trust. Humble yourself in the presence of one who is wise. Ask questions. Listening to key voices in your life will not only give you wisdom, but will also surround you with protection and blessing.

Over the past several years, different spiritual voices in my life have remarked, "Keith, your life and your family's life is a picture of divine acceleration. What has taken us years, you are walking into in months. You have the wisdom of a much older man." If that is true, it is only because I have learned to heed the advice and words of elders—

people to whom I listened and from whom I learned. Everything I have in this life is from the heavenly Father and earthly mothers and fathers. I cannot take credit, but I can be thankful. In all humility, we ought to produce greater things than the previous generation because we have squeezed every nugget of wisdom out of our inheritance.

It's not enough to simply acquire spiritual riches. You must also be sensitive to what the voice of wisdom has to say. I once heard about a man who wanted a key father in the faith to be his spiritual father. He telephoned this man and told him that he would like to meet with him. The potential father informed him that he could only meet at six o'clock that evening. The young man said he could not make it because of a previous engagement. The older father promptly hung up the phone. The young man called back and said, "I will be there at six o'clock."

Now this is an extreme example, but do you see my point? Valuable people do not feel the need to give away their precious gems to everyone. Matthew 7:6, *"Do not give dogs what is sacred; do not throw your pearls to pigs. If you do, they may trample them under their feet, and then turn and tear you to pieces."* Spiritual fathers and mothers do not want to invest in undisciplined people who will not value their wisdom and time. For example, even if you are feeling nervous when you're around a spiritual father, resist the urge to speak too much. You are there to listen! On the other hand, don't simply clam up and not share anything at all as that can be just as much of a hindrance.

There was a middle-aged man who asked me to speak into his life. I said I would be glad to do so, but each time we met, I couldn't get a word in edgewise. He jabbered continually. His mouth was like a motor without an off switch! Finally I said, "If your reason for meeting with me is just because you need a friend, I am happy to provide that. But if you are truly serious about me providing input in your life, you need to allow me the opportunity to speak." In other words, stop talking! Sadly, he did not like my proposition and never returned. He wanted input, but only on his terms. Since then, I have remained a friend to him, but he has chosen not to receive input that could have helped him rise to the next level.

Proverbs 17:28 says, *"Even a fool is thought wise if he keeps silent, and discerning if he holds his tongue."* The art of knowing when to talk and when to listen is imperative. It is a skill I continue to cultivate. Learning to listen to my wife has helped me a great deal in the art of communication. Let me just say that sensitivity to others is not a natural strength of mine, connecting on a heart level has required considerable effort. Heather has a much better understanding in this realm and I am so thankful for her. At times she has said things like, "Keith, you were talking too much there." "They were not ready for what you said." "You pushed them too far." "You need to be just a friend with them right now." Proverbs 18:22 says, *"He who finds a wife finds what is good and receives favor from the Lord."* One of the reasons blessing has been accelerated in my life has been my wonderful wife who has patiently taught me how to be an exceptional listener and showed me the importance of being sensitive to others. Whether it's a great spouse, or a relational coach, learning effective communication will help you advance on the road to your destiny.

I have known many people who want someone to speak into their lives, but they do not understand relational protocol. Someone who carries a spirit of rejection will in turn reject people by their behavior without even being consciously aware of it. They presume everyone is against them and that they are unwanted. It is only by stepping into the Father's love that this misperception can be overcome.

You may be wondering, "How do you attract fathers and mothers into your life when you need them to help you overcome these issues?" Certain people are able to understand you, your issues and your potential, and will embrace you from the start. I am grateful for the many who have done that for me. There are other people who do not possess the time or energy for extreme, unhealthy, relational behaviors. If you want to attract these voices into your life you must first address your insecurities and relational issues.

God knows what you need, who you need it from, how you can receive it and will entrust you with more and more input according to the needs of your calling. You can become a bulls-eye for blessing by learning to value the input and wisdom of those He brings your way... even though they may not be "world renowned." I strongly believe this key is one of the most significant ingredients to long-term success in your life and will be well worth the time and effort.

We have learned that in order to have ever-increasing blessing flowing in your life, you must be connected to fathers and mothers who will bestow inheritance through their words, relationships, prayer and care. Your destiny is connected to your level of identity. In the next chapter, I want to help you understand that to affect your generation you must know and embrace this identity.

Chapter 7

U.B.U.

Y ou will not realize the dreams of your heart until you allow your identity to emerge. In the last few chapters we learned that knowing who you are comes from allowing the heavenly Father and spiritual fathers to speak into your life. As I continued on this journey of allowing my identity to surface I realized the process involved in pursuing my dreams would be challenging as I learned to live for God's approval and not that of men. I did not realize that discovering my identity would be like peeling an onion. There were layers of fear I still had to expose in order to get to the core of who I truly was.

As mentioned previously, my over the top need for man's approval was like a ball and chain around my life. Encouraging words were so satisfying to hear that I didn't want to be in situations where I wouldn't be affirmed. I was all about being applauded and hearing people tell me what a great guy I was. This produced a belief that in order to be valued I had to give people what they wanted. As a result, allowing my true identity to emerge required courage—courage to reveal my unique, God-given design and to embrace the person He had made me to be.

One of the challenges came in the area of developing a willingness to travel different paths than those of my heroes. These were men and women who I admired and modeled my life after. Subtly, the aspiration to be like those I esteemed became a hindrance to stepping into my identity. It seemed at times as if I was trying to be like every single person I idolized. Basically, my entire life was one big act with me taking on the characteristics and personality traits of whomever I deemed the most influential at the moment. My congregation, pastoral friends and people in our community were all presented with a different personality depending on who I was with—one person, one personality; another person, another personality. It was like having a spiritual version of multiple personality disorder! As my true self began to emerge I fought constantly against the urge to shove it back down and revert to the crippling addiction to man's approval.

Living under the pressure of being esteemed by everyone and relating to them through a wrong view of 1 Corinthians 9:20-22 became unsustainable: *To the Jews I became like a Jew, to win the Jews. To those under the law I became like one under the law (though I myself am not under the law), so as to win those under the law. To those not having the law I became like one not having the law (though I am not free from God's law but am under Christ's law), so as to win those not having the law. To the weak I became weak, to win the weak. I have become all things to all people so that by all possible means I might save some.* Somehow I knew that living under my dysfunctional, self-imposed charade of adapting to everyone's comfort zones was not what Paul had in mind. It had to stop! But for me, walking in my identity as a free Son of God would only occur by way of humility.

One of our good friends, and a great model of the Father's love, Rich Oliver, was a catalyst in producing a bountiful harvest of freedom in my fearful heart. Rich and his wife, Lindy visited our church in Willits every year and were always a source of encouragement. On one visit they arrived shortly before I led a "joy walk" through the coastal towns of our region. The plan was to meet local intercessors along the way and walk together through the towns while celebrating the goodness of God. Each night we planned to meet in a local church, spending time in prayer for each town. This would take about a week to accomplish as we began about three hours north and worked our way down Highway 101 with the grand finale being in our hometown of Willits.

During the Olivers' visit I shared my struggles with Rich regarding my obsession with pleasing others. Rich said, "Keith, I have a suggestion for you. You need to wear something like a jester's hat during the course of this prayer walk. That will free you from the fear of man and break that dignified spirit off of you." Really? He wanted me to walk through my hometown—a place I now pastor and am generally well liked—wearing a jester's hat? As soon as he said this, scenarios of what the intercessors up north would think of me began running through my mind. Given that most of them were what I'd refer to as "depressed intercessors," their context for understanding what I was doing would either be non-existent or severely limited. How would they handle joyful intercession that cut directly against the grain of their spirit of heaviness?

Oddly enough, I had purchased a jester's hat for my children during a recent trip to England. Rich told me that in ancient times jesters, or "fools," played a significant role in the culture of nobility. Their job was to make the king happy, not an easy task since most kings were not easily humored. As a result, instead of humoring the king, some of the fools tried to humor the people who surrounded the king...much easier and much less pressure. Rich said that he felt I needed to settle the issue in my heart that I was a "fool" for the King and no one else. Of course this produced even more fear. To be quite honest, I was scared stiff!

The next day Rich and Lindy returned home while I traveled north with a few people from our local church. We drove three hours to the first town to commence the prayer walk. When we arrived, I pulled out my jester's hat and put it on. Sure enough, some of the intercessors we met were the serious ones—the ones I dreaded being around. I hated the thought of these grumpy, heavy-spirited people speaking out critically against me or mocking the "circus clown." I also didn't want to have to explain my reasoning and seek the approval of each person I met.

Some had a hard time understanding my actions, while others embraced what, in their eyes at least, was not normal prayer: Jumping around, celebrating wildly through the streets of the towns we visited. It may not sound like prayer to some, but I have observed many supernatural signs along with tremendous breakthrough following these kinds of walks.

There came a point during the walk through one city where we encountered resistance. It could have been resistance to our joy, or perhaps to the abnormal prayer of the dancing fools. The people we met to lead us around town did not enter in and it seemed as if our presence was seen very negatively. The severe controls they placed on the meeting that was to take place that evening—i.e. no "obnoxious praise" or joyful antics—effected me emotionally to the point that I became quite distraught. Nevertheless, I told our team that we would honor their wishes and hold to the values of esteeming others regardless of our differences.

I attended the meeting and several of the men from our team ended up in the restroom simultaneously. One of them approached me at the washbasin, grabbed a paper towel from the dispenser and put it over my face while saying, "Keith, the glory is so thick on you I have to cover your face." Keep in mind that I was determined to not create any waves during this meeting, but as soon as he placed the paper towel over my face I fell to the ground overcome by laughter. After repeatedly trying and failing to stand, I resorted to crawling out of the bathroom and down the hall. I inched my way toward the entrance, halting at the steps leading into the building. However, when I reached the steps I could go no farther and lay there the whole night laughing, which meant that everyone who attended the meeting had to walk over or around me to get in. The meeting went on and when it was over several of the leaders quietly came up to me and said, "Keith, can you pray for me? I want what you have." The Lord, in His way, taught me that when I am a fool for Him, people see Christ and desire that freedom.

The remainder of the prayer walk went well but in the back of my mind, I knew that Willits was coming—my home town, with its mile-long Main Street down which I would be skipping and jumping. That, my friends, was a whole new level of humility!

Heather had joined the team the day before we arrived in Willits and was struggling a bit with the foolish antics of the prayer walkers as we jumped up and down wildly praising and shouting God's name in the streets. As we approached Willits, with much fear and trembling I prepared myself to be a fool for Jesus. The Lord impressed on Heather's heart that instead of me wearing the hat through the town *she* should wear the hat. He told her that she needed to deal with her own fears and the need to be dignified. So she wore the colorful, bell-ringing jester's hat, dancing through the streets with the rest of us. When she finished, Heather returned to her workplace at the public school. Sure enough, one of the parents there had seen her on the streets and inquired about her outlandish behavior. Attracting the attention of people she knew was the very thing she had feared the most. But through this experience God helped her realize that she belonged to Him, regardless of what others say or think of us.

That prayer walk went a long way in freeing me from the need to live for the accolades of people. If you have a hard time receiving this story because you think, "That kind of noise in broad daylight is disrespectful and insensitive to others," I would wholeheartedly agree. I did not choose to do it this way, but it was the only way God could liberate me from chains that for so long had me bound. The bottom line is this: We must be willing to do whatever it takes to eradicate the fear of man. *You* must be willing to do it.

A political spirit requires people to tiptoe around cultural norms, not ruffling any feathers. While I am not into waving activist signs in the streets and being hostile toward government or city officials, there are times when God requires us, for the sake of the Kingdom, to stretch the boundaries of civil obedience. Take the issue that arose in Daniel 6. A law had been given that no one could worship God. But Daniel 6:10 says, *Now when Daniel learned that the decree had been published, he went home to his upstairs room where the windows opened toward Jerusalem. Three times a day he got down on his knees and prayed, giving thanks to his God, just as he had done before.* I love it! Prayer to all other gods has been forbidden and what does Daniel do? He goes home and where *everyone* can see him, thanks and praises God as usual. You would assume that acting in this fashion wouldn't exactly curry favor with the government, but when Daniel was punished in accordance with the king's own law, it was the king himself who tried to find a way to rescue him. When Daniel emerged unscathed from the lion's den, the king ordered the whole nation to fear and revere the God of Daniel. Instead of this highly visible, radical praise causing Daniel's God to be reviled, it actually increased God's renown. It also caused Daniel to prosper and increase in favor in his governmental position.

Recently the Lord told me to undertake another joy walk. This time it was to be in the town where I currently reside, Vacaville, California. Unbeknownst to me, that same dignified spirit had crept in, attempting to steal the full impact of who I am and compromise my ability to penetrate my culture. 2 Tim. 1:7 says, *"For God did not give us a spirit of timidity, but a spirit of power, of love and of self-discipline."* The word "timidity" means fear, but it also means, "To be a little less than who you are." The enemy does not mind if we are Christians, or even if we worship, as long as we keep the fire of worship in the "fireplace" and not release it beyond the four walls of our churches. He doesn't mind if we serve Christ as long as we do not outrageously love Him and others — as long as we are quiet and just a *little less* than who we are meant to be, conforming to the masses and not ruffling any feathers.

David understood that pleasing God would often cost you something. In 1 Chronicles 21:24 he says, *"No, I insist on paying the full price. I will not take for the Lord what is yours, or sacrifice a burnt offering that costs me nothing."* Then, when David had the privilege of returning the Ark of the Presence to Israel he worshiped the Lord passionately, dancing wildly, extravagantly through the streets of Jerusalem incurring the displeasure of his wife, Michel. In 2 Samuel 6:22, David says in reply to her complaint, *"I will become even more undignified than this, and I will be humiliated in my own eyes. But by these slave girls you spoke of, I will be held in honor."*

The Apostle Paul shares God's thought about David in Acts 13:22, *"After removing Saul, he made David their king. He testified concerning him: 'I have found David son of Jesse a man after my own heart; he will do everything I want him to do.'"* David, imperfect though he may have been, was a man after God's heart and the Lord chose to establish His rule on the throne of David. If we want to affect our generation, hear God say the same things about us, we must be willing to receive and agree with the words of identity He speaks over us.

I have heard it said, "You are a terrible copy, but a great you." When we try to mimic what everyone else does, we are not very spectacular. You are the only *you* that God has created. You are uniquely designed. No one else can praise the Lord the way you do. No one else has the gifting, calling, characteristics, unique experiences or encounters with God and man that you have. You are wonderfully distinct!

Heather has a wonderful message about "being you" that has been birthed out of her own life's journey. When she speaks this message she will tell people, "U.B.U." These letters stand for, "You Be You." As I tried again and again to become who God specifically created me to be, she would often remark, "Keith, you are a terrible '_____' but you are a great you." I respected so many people that I wanted to be like them. I am a musician and in my music I often sounded and played like someone I admired. I would see a speaker I admired and attempt to emulate them. I would think of all those heroes who had gone before me and I wanted to be like them. While I am thankful for the things they all taught and provoked in me, God was up to something else. Heather would say in regards to people I tried to emulate, "Keith, you are not a Keith Green. You are not a Bill Johnson. You are not a Lindell Cooley…U.B.U., Keith."

One of the main ways we begin to step into our identity is through an understanding of our uniqueness as sons and daughters. I shared in a previous chapter that fathers bring identity. The heavenly Father speaks identity into us as well. These words of identity not only form who we are, they call *forth* who we really are.

Gideon was hiding in a winepress, threshing wheat in fear for his life, when the Angel of the Lord came and declared his identity to him. Judges 6:11-12, *"The angel of the Lord came and sat down under the oak in Ophrah that belonged to Joash the Abiezrite, where his son Gideon was threshing wheat in a winepress to keep it from the Midianites. When the angle of the Lord appeared to Gideon, he said, 'The Lord is with you, mighty warrior.'"* Gideon stepped out of that place of fear and into his identity, leading the army of Israel to an amazing, supernatural victory. As a result of his courageous actions, birthed out of knowing and embracing who God said he was, Israel remained free from oppression for forty years.

Before Jesus completed one bit of ministry, His heavenly Father spoke to his identity. Matthew 3:17, *"And a voice from heaven said, 'This is my Son, whom I love; with him I am well pleased.'"* That identity not only sustained Him through His time of testing with the devil but also propelled Him into a ministry of power. Notice in Matthew 4:3, the devil immediately went after Jesus' identity. *"The tempter came to him and said, 'If you are the Son of God, tell these stones to become bread.'"* He was trying to make Jesus prove His identity instead of walking in the power of His identity. The devil tempted Him again, and once again Jesus spoke from His identity. *"'It is also written: 'Do not put the Lord your God to the test.'"* (Matthew 4:7) I do not have to prove anything to you, devil! The Father has already told me that I am His son and that is enough. Jesus allowed His identity as Son to release Him into His destiny.

In reply to His critics, Jesus said that He only did what He saw the Father doing. John 5:19, *"Jesus gave them this answer: 'I tell you the truth, the Son can do nothing by himself; he can do only what he sees his Father doing, because whatever the Father does the Son also does.'"* Everything He did came out of His identity as a son.

As a result of being at The Mission Vacaville, I have developed an "Identity Statement" by using a process they developed. My statement has continued to grow and evolve as the Lord upgrades my identity. I now have about three pages of things that have been spoken to me by the Lord and through various prophetic words. These sentences define my identity as a son and now hang by my bathroom mirror where I can see and declare them over myself regularly.

Here is a small sample of my Identity Statement.

I am a believer who agrees with heaven's declarations without toiling for the fulfillment of those promises. I am a new creation, pure in every way, madly in love with my spouse, Heather. I am a team player with my wife and many others, embracing and enjoying their strengths, differences, and weaknesses. I am a saint, a holy believer. I am faithful and trustworthy. I am a friend worthy of friends. I am a person of courage, fearless before the enemy, a person of joy, an overcomer of obstacles and a favored well pleasing son unconditionally loved and accepted as I am. I am a new creation. I am a good Father...

I have found that the more I live from a place of true identity, the more secure I am and there is greater authority in my walk, my life and my words. I am more at peace and the fear of man does not have the hold on me it had before.

My Identity Statement has become a source of strength to me because it is who God says I am, which encourages me to move into places of my dreams and destiny. When I am called upon to minister in power, I declare over myself, *I am a person of healing, I carry a signs and wonders anointing, heavens open, Kingdoms shake and God's Kingdom comes wherever I go.* When I enter an unfamiliar situation I declare over myself, *I do not walk in a spirit of foreboding fear but I am a person of hope. I live with an expectation and excitement of good coming my way.* When I enter a roomful of great leaders, among whom I could feel intimidated, I declare over myself, *I am not inferior to any authorities, whether the rich, political leaders, church leaders, or people of influence. Together we stand alongside of each other serving God alone, while honoring one another.*

As I have continued to rehearse these declarations daily, my actions have begun to follow suit. Instead of trying to fit into every situation I come into, I embrace the truth that I am uniquely and wonderfully made.

I declare over myself, *I am real, living out loud, nothing hidden in my life. My worship, affection, and love for my family and God are always the same. I don't cater to crowds. I am who I am in every situation. The just* *shall live by being **real**. I am a reformer who lives my life as a model of the new day of living real. I am real in youth meetings, churches with different wineskins, city atmospheres and among the lost. I am authentically me in worship leading, preaching and relationships. I am not living behind the walls of fear that people won't accept me. I am living out loud. My songs bring God praise because they are genuinely mine.*

I am not in the market for "typical" meetings; those have already been over-done. In every situation I am always who I am and always allow the Holy Spirit to be who He is. I am breaking out of the shell of conformity and niceness. I am a prophetic voice to the nations declaring that God values you as you are. I am truly accepted and loved as I am before him. My writings, songs, worship and teachings all come from a place of authenticity. Authenticity is a core value of mine that must be lived out everywhere I go. I am not called to fit into every crowd...I am called to be myself in every situation.

You too can develop your own Identity Statement. Take all the words God says you are, along with the significant prophetic words God has given you and work through them with a few friends finding everything that God says you are. You need the help of friends because often times as we begin to embrace our destiny we do not yet perceive ourselves the way God perceives us.

The way we hold each other accountable to the great things God says about us is reminding each other of who we are, saying things like, "You are way too amazing to act like that. You are a world changer." When Heather and I speak into our children, often after they have blundered, we say, "Son, daughter, you are a prince, a princess and you are way too awesome to be acting less than that."

In the same way that the angel's declaration catapulted Gideon into his identity as a mighty warrior — the prince who saved a nation — understanding your identity will propel you toward your destiny as a world changer for the Kingdom.

Becoming a person who does not settle for less takes great courage. In the next chapter I want to dive deeper into the subject of dealing with fear. We will go after the spirit of courage that is needed to step into a powerful and supernatural lifestyle.

Nothing less will do than you being fully you in every situation.

U.B.U!

Chapter 8

From Cowardly Lion to Braveheart

A few years ago I received a prophetic word that said, "The Lord's name for you is 'Courage.'" When I heard those words, my immediate response was, "That certainly isn't me!" It would prove to be quite a journey to step into that part of my identity, for fear had become my normal. Beyond my own personal struggle, fear also seemed the weapon of choice used to strong-arm people into obedience in church settings.

My view of God contributed in part to this stronghold. I imagined God as the strong, disciplinary type; a distant, cold being to be approached with foreboding. This was the filter through which I tended to view all of life. Whether it involved vocalizing my faith in God or expecting maltreatment for my beliefs, I was overwhelmed by my rapidly growing fears—fears that I knew I would have to tackle.

As a child I had been taught that serving Jesus would almost certainly result in persecution for your faith. Even at a young age I did many things for the Lord publicly, but always with a constant fear of rejection. My demonstrative and dramatic encounters with God created waves of friction. Although that was not a pleasant thought, I have come to realize that every time you step into something new, others will need understanding to help them come into agreement with your encounter. My attempts to avoid deception and ensure that every encounter was truly Biblical created constant pressure. This atmosphere was riddled with suspicion of anything or anyone outside my grid of understanding.

It seemed like I was trapped in a prison with no way out.

Having a spiritual sensitivity to certain atmospheres created even more fear because I had no training in the art of living a supernatural life in the world. Everything I felt in the natural realm became my burden in the Spiritual realm. The only way I would take a stand of opposition was when something stood against my personal beliefs. I did not have a working understanding of particular spiritual climates. For example, I did not realize that the spirit of fear often resided in certain atmospheres and cultures of people; thus, these burdens transferred easily to my heart and mind and I lacked the tools to ward them off. Needless to say, becoming free of the stronghold of fear required nothing less than the supernatural intervention of God.

There were a number of factors that combined to create my stronghold of fear: A wrong view of God; a lack of trust in His protection; a flawed eschatology and a lack of true fathering needed to create a sense of safety, protection and trust. Little by little, God began to crack my fearful heart. As I shared in earlier chapters, He revealed fatherly love to me by sending earthly fathers who tangibly demonstrated His love. This became a fortress of strength for me and allowed me to develop new levels of trust in my walk with God.

As this journey toward freedom continued God began to draw me into the place of facing my fears.

One day that proved to be a significant part of my path toward liberty is forever etched in my heart. On that particular morning I sensed the Lord telling me that I needed to go to a local walking trail at nine o'clock. This was a walking/running course that I frequented when I wanted to exercise and be alone with God. Set in the mountains, it wound through creeks and beautiful redwood trees creating a wonderful retreat.

I arrived at nine a.m. As soon as I pulled into the parking lot another car containing a man and woman pulled in as well. I immediately sensed that this was no coincidence and felt there may be a conversation in store between these complete strangers and myself.

They started walking and I followed them around the course asking the Lord what I was supposed to say to them. I sensed Him saying that I should prophesy to them, only it was to be in a way that was totally abnormal for me, i.e. prophesying without first making their acquaintance. I wasn't even supposed to find out if they were Christians or not, but simply walk up to them and say, "Thus saith the Lord." This was not something I routinely did, because I had learned that if you are too direct with prophecy it can be distasteful or even offensive to people. Also, prefacing a prophetic word with, "Thus saith the Lord" doesn't leave a lot of room for the word to be tested. However, on this particular morning He wanted me to do exactly that. And I knew it. The Lord's promise to me was, "If you do this, I will break fear off your life." As I continued walking around the course my mind raced. *What will they say? What if I'm wrong? I'll look so stupid! Surely that wasn't God speaking. It must be my own thinking...*on and on the thoughts continued. You know those thoughts...the ones that enter your mind when you step out for God in a new way. It is as though every available demon shows up simultaneously on the scene to torment you.

Several years prior to this, the Lord had told me that, like David, after I had faced the lion and the bear in my life, I would get my chance at Goliath. The lion and the bear were pictures of accusation and temptation; Goliath was representative of fear. Like Goliath, fear loomed tall, dark and intimidating, yelling its lies at me. *Who do you think you are little boy? You will look very foolish when you step out and you know it.* Around and around those thoughts continued to race. I desperately tried to gain the courage to approach this couple and speak to them. It was like trying to get the courage to jump off a high diving board: "Ready? 1, 2, 3, jump! No, I can't! Okay, yes I will. 1, 2, 3, jump!" Well, that's exactly where I was. "1, 2, 3, prophesy! No, I can't! Okay, yes I will.1, 2, 3, prophesy! No, I can't! Okay, yes I will.1, 2, 3, prophesy!" It was a battle.

As I continued this internal conflict, frozen at the intersection of choice, I saw the couple heading toward their car. "Will I choose to prophesy, or will I walk off the diving board in defeat...again?" The couple stood at their car with the doors swung and open about to step in while I walked toward my vehicle. All I knew was that I might never see this couple again. How many opportunities of blessing have I missed because of my lack of courage? Would this be another opportunity or would I rise up and give God glory by delivering the prophetic mail he wanted me to deliver? I blurted out, "Excuse me. I have a word from God for the both of you."

They stopped dead in their tracks and the man turned toward me. Would I be rejected? Would I be told to take a hike? The woman stepped out of the car and faced me with a serious but intent look. I said, "I don't normally do this, but God has a word for you." I proceeded to share the word of the Lord with them, which took quite a while. With the woman weeping, I prayed for both of them. Eventually I discovered she had cancer, and again, I prayed.

After parting, I sat in my car, awestruck by the faithfulness of the Lord. I was in high heaven, praising and thanking God. Goliath and I had faced off; I looked him straight in the eye and took him down with one shot. Victory! I had a word from God: If I prophesied, fear would be broken off my life. I *had* prophesied and, indeed, fear had been broken off my life. The heavens opened as Goliath fell hard to the ground...dead in his tracks.

On my way home that day I stopped at the church so I could spend a few hours in a quiet place. Revelation leaped off the page at me from the Word of God. I saw visions from heaven. I was free. Then I headed to my home adjacent to the church. When I stepped outside, I looked up and saw a beautiful, blue sky through a circle in the clouds that seemed situated directly over our house. I knew this meant we literally had an open heaven over our home. I ran inside shouting, "You have to come outside right now and ask God for anything you want. We have an open heaven." Heather and the kids joined me. My daughter, who was four years old at the time was immediately filled with the Holy Spirit, laughing and speaking in a heavenly language, all without any coaching from Heather or me. As soon as she was filled, the power of God hit me and I fell into what we call "the spiritual crunches," bent over under the power of God, bobbing up and down and laughing. For weeks we would enter Maci's room at night and she would break out in tongues and laughter. What a momentous time for my family!

The Lord taught me so much that day. Fear had been like a restrictive ceiling over our household, but as the head of my family when I became free, the heavens opened up. It was sobering to understand that if you live long enough under the spirit of fear it becomes a "familiar spirit" completely at home in your midst. The act of tackling the spirit itself can take only a moment in time, but to actually create and sustain a mindset that does not welcome fear is a process involving battles that must be fought until the foe is vanquished. You must fight until fear has nowhere to land in your life, nowhere to lodge its snare of death. Fear is like the ant. You can kill one, but if you have food lying on the ground the community of ants will eventually return regardless of how much poison you spray. You must keep your "house" clean, free from the fearful thoughts that attract the demonic to return again and again and again. After that dramatic moment, I walked free from fear and never looked back.

I was on a journey to learn how to prophesy to people and minister in healing regardless of location or circumstances. I encountered some challenges, but there were many breakthroughs, which served to fuel my engine of increased faith. As time went on I entered a six-month season when every person I offered to pray for told me to go away, that they weren't interested, or something of that nature. I hated rejection and this process of rejection was dreadful. Nobody got healed...and I felt little power.

During that time healing and deliverance ministers, Bill and Carol Dew, visited for a weekend and I took the opportunity to share my struggles in this area. We saw a lady walking with a cast who obviously needed healing. When I approached her and offered prayer, she responded with a strong, "No!" Bill said to me, "You sure have that rejection thing badly, don't you?" Carol encouraged me to keep pressing in sensing that God wanted to give me a double portion in this area. Even if people said "No!" the heavens were getting holes poked in them every time we prayed for someone. That was encouraging, but I still needed a major breakthrough.

One day I traveled to the coast, which was about forty-five minutes away from Willits. I love the beach because it is one place where I seem able to encounter God in special ways. There is something about the ocean waves and their crashing sound, the soft sand and sweet smell, that never gets old. While standing on the shoreline God said, "Keith, I want to give you back your mantle of power. You lost it a while ago when you started fearing rejection. Just as love casts out fear, fear can cast out power." The Lord said that He would restore the power, but I would have to safeguard it. I got the power back that day and resolved in my spirit that I would never allow it to be kidnapped again. Ever!

I'd love to say that it was easy to pray for people on the streets after that, but it was some time before things got better. I'd also love to say that I never again gave into fear. Sadly, in many instances I did. But I now embraced by faith my new name, "Courage," and it was something I would have to grow into. In the journey to my new identity, the Lord taught me that it was not enough to simply confront the spirit of fear, but that I must also build a stronghold of courage. He taught me how to respond immediately to His Spirit. Kris Vallotton once said, "Courage is faith in the face of fear. Faith is spelled R-I-S-K. It takes courage to step out in faith and take a risk."

One day while traveling down the hill that led into our city, I had a vision of a police officer beating his wife. The next thing you know, I drove past a police car hidden on the side of the road. The officer was pointing his speed gun at the passing cars and I knew I was supposed to talk to him. "I can't go up to him, Lord, and tell him to stop beating his wife! What am I supposed to do?" On a side note, I was in a season where I was learning that the role of prophecy was to encourage others. Even if you hear something perceived as negative in the spirit, you need to find the heart of the Lord in that word to encourage others. If there is a sin issue present, we are taught to speak to the solution...not to the problem. Whatever you speak life into will grow.

The Lord and I worked it out. I turned my car around, drove right up to the police car, excused myself and told the man that God was giving him a new, amazing ability to be gentle with his wife. Giving that word was a little scary, but sharing it with a police officer was even more frightening. The Lord didn't seem to mind. You see, He was going after my own fear of man and was using this strange situation as a way to provoke me to face those fears.

So often in those days I looked for a perfect scenario before I would approach anyone in public with a word of prophecy. I would make sure no one else was around so that if I made a mistake I wouldn't look foolish in front of others. I would size up the person to determine whether he or she would be receptive to my offer. Sounds like the thinking of someone dealing with the fear of rejection to me...

I went into a store one afternoon and overheard a woman saying that she was in pain. As soon as I heard it, I knew I should pray for her. I thoroughly assessed my surroundings and determined that it was *not* the perfect scenario. She was one of the workers at the store and there were too many people around. So I left the building and drove away without doing anything. Instantly, I was overtaken and overwhelmed by the Holy Spirit *and* guilt! I'm not suggesting that they are one and the same; it's just that at the time, I could not distinguish between the two. Guilt told me what a terrible person I was for missing that opportunity, while the Holy Spirit gently nudged me to return and finish the work. The Lord is so patient, continually working with us to step into the place of ministry He provides for us.

I turned the car around, returned to the store and headed straight for the woman. After locating her I said, "I overheard you talking about having pain in your body. Can I pray for you?" She agreed and I proceeded to pray for her. She was very touched by my gesture and when I returned on another visit, she thanked me profusely for what I had done for her.

As I grew in the prophetic, I discovered that people are generally touched that you care enough to pray for them, as long as it's authentic.

If however, you carry a spirit of rejection into a prophetic situation and the other person is also carrying that same spirit, it will rise up and cause them to feel rejection from you. Much like dogs that smell fear and go after the one that is afraid, when we sense the spirit of rejection in somebody our natural reaction is to reject them thereby losing an opportunity for relationship and blessing. In order to eventually see breakthrough that spirit must be defeated.

As you can see, breaking free from a fear-filled mindset was not a one-time shot. Even though the Lord gave me life-changing encounters to develop courage, I had much to conquer in this arena. King David walked a similar path as he learned to overcome fear in his own life. At a young age he developed a courageous spirit as he witnessed and understood God's faithful interventions in his life. His defeat of the lion and the bear allowed him to confront Goliath when everyone else was afraid.

1 Samuel 17:34-36 But *David said to Saul, "Your servant has been keeping his father's sheep. When a lion or a bear came and carried off a sheep from the flock, I went after it, struck it and rescued the sheep from its mouth. When it turned on me, I seized it by its hair, struck it and killed it. Your servant has killed both the lion and the bear; this uncircumcised Philistine will be like one of them, because he has defied the armies of the living God.*

David took the testimonies of his past victories in God with him as he confronted a man who brandished fear like a weapon over the entire Israeli army. 1 Samuel 17:24 says, *"When the Israelites saw the man, they all ran from him in great fear."* I love David's story because it illustrates what one courageous warrior can overcome even when everyone else is under the spirit of intimidation. As the story continues, 1 Samuel 17:50 says, *"So David triumphed over the Philistine with a sling and a stone; without a sword in his hand he struck down the Philistine and killed him."*

This was a turning point for the nation of Israel. This young man's one act of fearless faith made him a hero and produced breakthrough, which restored the hope of an entire nation. One would think that all was well, but this was just the starting point for David. His courage brought him before King Saul, but the same tenacious faith that caused the people to love and admire David, ultimately caused Saul to envy him. 1 Samuel 18:7-8, *"As they danced, they sang; "Saul has slain his thousands and David his tens of thousands; Saul was very angry; this refrain galled him."*

David realized that if he didn't "get out of Dodge," Saul would eventually kill him. But where could he go? What possible place existed where Saul could not reach him? 1 Samuel 21:10, *"That day David fled from Saul and went to Achish King of Gath."* What a place for David to flee...right into the enemy's camp, the same enemy that was the source of Israel's stronghold of fear. David eventually became a resident of Gath along with his six hundred warriors. 1 Samuel 27:2-3, *"So David and the six hundred men with him left and went over to Achish son of Maok King of Gath. David and his men settled in Gath with Achish."* David remained in the camp for several years until Saul was killed.

In time, David became king and fought against the very ones who had given him refuge, ultimately gaining victory over the Philistines and the fear they represented. Clearly, David's circumstances got worse before they got better. He was a courageous warrior but had to tackle fear, rejection and anger on many levels. He experienced success as well as failure, both of which were necessary in forming in him the strength and resolve necessary to rule Israel.

"Courageous," means having faith in the face of fear. However, we are not called to merely be courageous...we are called to be conquering warriors. It is possible to be courageous and still not overcome your enemy. You faced him, but he took you down. David had to learn how to maintain a courageous attitude until he increased enough in strength to throw off the fears that not only compromised the success of his life but also those under his rule.

As we become more adept at facing and overcoming fears, our identity moves from "courageous warrior" to "conquering warrior." We are not meant to just be good fighters...we are meant to be victorious. If you are a warrior who conquers and occupies land in the spirit realm the Lord grants you, it means you must remain consistently confident in the Lord's love and goodness, trusting in His care for you.

As you break out of the mindset that says, "Only bad things happen to me!" it is crucial to replace that stronghold with hope. Hope is the expectation and excitement of good things coming your way. Not only do you want to eliminate the fear of rejection or bad things coming your way, you want to create an expectation of good things in store for your life. When you enter places that normally intimidate you, you must declare and expect good things to meet you there. Expect breakthroughs, receptivity, open doors, friendships, supernatural encounters, favor and blessing to cross your path. Declare over your future that it is *good* and that you are excited to see what God has in store for you. Be joyfully expectant.

Another key to dealing with fear is to diligently keep your heart at peace. In my formative years being "salt and light" wasn't something we learned. We treated the world as something to be feared instead of seeing it as an opportunity to advance the Kingdom. As a result I learned to be wary of new age cults and other religions. The town in which I lived had a new age and Wiccan stronghold over it. As time went on, I met some new agers and Wiccans and even invited several to our church.

One day I entered a new age store and noticed that there were several idols on the shelves. You could feel the heaviness in the air and my immediate response was fear. I had just prayed for the owner of this store on a street corner and he had been healed. He was hungry for what I carried and yet I was afraid to step foot in his store. As I wrestled with my fears the Lord said, "Hold your peace." A light clicked on for me. If I did not allow the enemy to manipulate me through fear, he would not have access to me. The presence of evil was not due to the absence of God, but *because* God was with me. I held my peace and over time continued to be an influence in that businessperson's life and family.

Another episode drove this home a little deeper when I was asked to conduct the funeral of a Native American. I did not know him personally, but his brother was a believer and had invited me to officiate the funeral. The service was performed on tribal land and had barely gotten underway when several Native Americans stormed in and interrupted the meeting to do a "smudging" ritual (consisting of burning certain herbs and brushing the smoke over the body). Up to that point there had been a strong sense of God's presence and peace but when they entered the room the atmosphere filled with fear...perhaps my own. I felt the Lord say again, "Just watch and see what happens." They performed their ceremony and when they left the presence of the Lord not only returned, but increased. God was teaching me to trust Him. By holding my peace, fear had no capacity to cripple me from walking in my authority.

I am still on the journey to becoming a fearless warrior; full of excitement and the expectation that good is coming my way. Although fear attempts to creep in now and then, it is no longer my comrade. We have walked through this process of journeying out of the stronghold of fear and into a courageous life. In the next chapter I want to explore what is required in order to become a person of power; a person through whom God can move fearlessly in extraordinary signs and wonders.

Chapter 9

You Can Fly

God used my cry for "more" as a catalyst to launch me into a greater awareness of His power. I grew up feeling confident that I knew what it meant to be a Christian, walking in everything that was available in God and assuming that I had arrived at the pinnacle of spirituality. I spoke in tongues, prayed, evangelized, led my local youth group in preaching and worship, and I publicly spoke in other church venues, all before the age of twenty. Despite this, the Lord increased the desire in my heart for a greater manifestation of Kingdom expression here on earth.

One day while attending Bible College, I sat quietly studying the Word, pondering the lives of people in the Bible. I noticed many of them were moving in greater power than I had ever experienced. Something in my heart cried out, "There must be more than what I am currently experiencing!" I began to question whether I was really filled with the Spirit even though my leaders told me I was. The Lord was definitely up to something.

At that same time the power of God was breaking out in incredible ways all over the earth. These powerful moves—characterized by the Father drawing His people back to their first love—were shaking the church. The power of God has always moved throughout the earth, but there was a great need for an awakening to the lack of love and power in the global body of Christ. I had no context within which I could understand what was happening. As previously mentioned, I had initially stood against these moves of God, rejecting and renouncing them simply because they didn't fit my definition of what constituted an acceptable spiritual encounter.

I feared spiritual deception, as did many of the leaders I esteemed. While expressions of the move we were seeing hadn't been spelled out chapter and verse in the Bible, they were certainly not new to God. In fact, the outbreak of God's power was a standard of the early church. My stumbling block had to do with the fact that what God was doing remained outside my understanding and control. I had determined that the manifestations were not "decently and in order," thus, it couldn't be on God's menu of spiritual blessings.

A powerless life is a joyless life, and a joyless life isn't exactly something that unbelievers find attractive. Historically, guilt and shame have been the tools used to gather people into the Kingdom. In fact, fear of punishment and hell has been a *primary* tool. What I, along with many others, failed to realize is that the power of God initiated by His love and compassion is the only thing that will bring in the great end time harvest.

While growing up I experienced the power of God, but only on special occasions and typically through "special" men and woman who we titled "evangelists." They would hold three or four days of revival meetings designed to excite the church and gather the lost. I recall seeing people falling under the power of God, laughing, crying, being healed and prophesied over in these meetings. But when the evangelist left town, although we remained excited for weeks following, we knew that the "revival" was over until the next visit, which, over time simply did not satisfy our souls. Though unintentional, this produced a belief that the *more* of God was only available through select messengers set apart for this divine purpose, while the rest of us were relegated to a life of fervently praying for God to visit while awaiting the arrival of the next messenger. In short, we did not understand that God's mighty power was available to everyone.

Despite the rigid encumbrance of my belief system, God invaded my life with His unrelenting love, freeing me from fear and causing me to see myself as a person of courage. As a result, I embarked on an amazing journey in the power of the Holy Spirit. I confronted fear, boldly faced rejection and grew in wisdom and knowledge of how to walk in the miraculous. As I continued to grow and develop the life of a courageous believer I stepped into higher dimensions—into a place above fear where only simple obedience and yielding to Him existed.

When Kim Clement, a well known prophet, was asked why his prophecies were so powerful—why he had the ability to address so many controversial issues with governments and leaders—he said that after struggling with fear for many years, he finally stopped caring what man thought about him. It was then, and only then that the Lord gave him the kind of powerful prophecies he delivers today. This is a great lesson for believers: A fearless person is dangerous to the works of darkness. Acts 10:37-38 says, *You know what has happened throughout the province of Judea...how God anointed Jesus of Nazareth with the Holy Spirit and power, and how he went around doing good and healing all who were under the power of the devil, because God was with him.*

As the Lord continued to teach me how to move into His might and counsel, He also provided practical experiences. One morning while driving down from my house in the mountains I had a vision of an elderly woman named Davida who had attended our church for some time and who, because of age, had become housebound. I suddenly felt an extreme urgency to visit her and made arrangements to do so that afternoon. A woman named Carol served as Davida's caregiver. Now, Carol had some very strange views about life and was given to ranting about the existence of UFO's and conspiracy theories regarding American presidents and the United States government. While I was visiting Davida that afternoon, Carol went off on one of her rants. Under the Holy Spirit's prompting, I suddenly and quite boldly found myself saying, "Carol, the issue is not any of the matters you have shared. The real issue is that you need to forgive your husband for abusing you." She began to weep and pour out her heart about her husband's abuse. I had no prior knowledge of her marital issues, but God used me to lead her to a place of forgiveness and into a relationship with Jesus that day. What a great lesson from my Master Teacher.

Moving in the Spirit of might and counsel means that you release the power of God whenever and wherever needed and possess the wisdom to witness God's power touch each situation uniquely and specifically. God's power backed by wisdom brings the necessary breakthrough and blessing for each person or situation you encounter.

On another occasion, I received a call from a physician friend of mine who worked in the Sacramento area, a three-hour drive from our home. He told me that a young woman under his care was close to death and requested my help. The woman's distressed family had been informed that she would not live through the night and he felt I could be of comfort to them. I agreed to come. Heather and I had only been on the road a short time when I was struck with a sickness so severe that we had to stop and pray for relief. Quite obviously the devil was attempting to halt something significant that God wanted to accomplish that day.

When we arrived, introductions were made and the family gathered around me, anxiously awaiting my words. I told them that I had not come to pray a "sympathy prayer" over their loved one, but had come to lay a bomb on the devil. The woman next to me exclaimed, "A bomb?!" "Yes!" I said. "We are in a battle. We are dealing with an enemy who is destroying your loved one's life." While I wouldn't normally declare such bold statements, when you respond in God's Spirit of might and counsel He gives you words that push the envelope.

I continued boldly, "This is the strategy: I will take three or four people with me who believe that the Lord can heal her. While in the room we are going to pray one at a time for her healing." Due to a drug overdose the young woman's liver count was alarmingly low and other functions in her body had shut down completely. She lay comatose in a portion of the room with absolutely no privacy. I instructed the family members who were present to start praying while I informed the boyfriend he needed to repent for living in sin with his girlfriend. Normally I wouldn't be so blunt with an unbeliever, but in that particular situation my bold instructions were part of the Lord's strategy to close a door the enemy had used to wreak havoc on this young woman's life.

I told the grandfather that he needed to release a blessing over his granddaughter. Her aunt, a pastor's wife and a nurse, began to repent for not asking the Lord for help and relying on medicine alone. Sometimes when I'm under the anointing my head shakes violently, which is unusual and unsightly for many. It's not what I choose, but when God moves I submit all of my being, including bodily control. Later on a nurse commented to my friend, "I didn't know white men could move that fast," referring to my headshake. That gave me a good chuckle. We prayed for the young lady until I felt a spirit of peace settle in the room. She did not emerge from the coma and there were no observable physical signs of change, but I knew we were done for the moment. So I spent time ministering to her family before we left.

A few days later my friend called to say that after I left the young woman came out of the coma, her liver count returned to normal and her other organs began to function again. The physicians in charge of her care called it a "miracle." When I later visited the young woman and her family, I learned that the boyfriend had given his life to the Lord and was making plans to serve God. Others in the family returned to the Lord as well. What a great opportunity that was to witness the result of the Spirit of might and counsel operating in a desperate situation.

That is how the Spirit of might and counsel works within us. At times it causes you to confront a situation completely counter to what the atmosphere seems to dictate. Moving in the Spirit of might and counsel is a unique and powerful way God breaks through resistance from those who oppose the power of God. It takes a person who knows how to yield to God without the intimidation of man to walk in this incredible release of power that is so needed in the earth!

Samson is an excellent example of someone who moved in the Spirit of might and counsel. Set apart by God from birth, he was trained at a young age to respond to the nudges of the Spirit. Judges 13:24-25 says, *"The woman gave birth to a boy and named him Samson. He grew and the Lord blessed him, and the Spirit of the Lord began to stir him."* Before he confronted the powers that bound the people of God, he learned to respond to the stirrings of the Spirit.

Many believers desire to walk in extraordinary power; to see the dead raised, the lame walk and cancer healed. However, if you want these miracles to be a normal part of life, you must start by being faithful in every situation that presents itself to you. When someone has a headache treat it as if it were cancer and pursue it no matter the cost. There is no difference between cancer and a headache in God's eyes — both were defeated at the cross. Sadly, our view has been compromised to the point that we see cancer as a daunting giant, while a headache is something to be tolerated. However, we must go after the Lord's heart for every sickness, disease or oppression of the enemy that comes our way. 1 Peter 2:24 says, *"...By his wounds you have been healed."* That settles it for me!

Jesus won the victory on the cross for every disease, sickness and oppression and it is my job to release that victory. I am called to treat works of the enemy in the same way as Jesus who wholeheartedly pursued and destroyed them. The key to learning to destroy *every* work of the enemy is responding in the seemingly small things. If you wait for the "big one" you will not have the necessary strength, confidence and courage to face it. As you look at the life of Jesus, you will recognize that the miracles He performed grew in magnitude and significance as His three years of ministry progressed. In the same way Jesus' ministry grew in power, so did Samson's.

After he learned to respond to the stirrings of the Spirit there came a moment when Samson was confronted by a lion. Judges 14:5-6, *Samson went down to Timnah together with his father and mother. As they approached the vineyards of Timnah, suddenly a young lion came roaring toward him. The Spirit of the LORD came upon him in power so that he tore the lion apart with his bare hands as he might have torn a young goat. But he told neither his father nor his mother what he had done.*

If you respond with the Spirit of God in small matters, when "giants" arise, you will know how to release the vastness of God's power to overcome that situation as well, which is exactly what Samson learned to do. He didn't operate in natural strength, but in the supernatural power of God moving through a vessel yielded to Him. As time progressed the same thing happened with increasing frequency and greater breakthrough.

Through the Spirit of might and counsel Samson killed thirty men to repay a debt and then caught three hundred foxes, tied their tails together in pairs, set their tails on fire and released them into an enemy's field. While each successive action launched him into a greater realm of opposition, he was still able to confront and defeat the enemy because he was yielded to the Spirit of God. His devotion caused his fear-based countrymen to eventually bind him and hand him over to the enemy. But the Spirit of God flooded Samson causing him to rip his ropes apart, grab a donkey's jawbone and kill a thousand men. What a feat of power. Wow! And all of this began by learning to respond to the stirrings of the Spirit.

"Well," you may think. "That was then and this is now. Power like that may have been needed in Biblical times, but now we can solve problems politely and calmly." I can guarantee that being nice will never advance the Kingdom. Matthew 11:12 in the King James Version says, *"And from the days of John the Baptist until now the kingdom of heaven suffereth violence, and the violent take it by force."* The enemy has always vehemently resisted the plans of God on the earth by seeking whom he may kill and devour. John 10:10 says, *"The thief comes only to steal and kill and destroy; I have come that they may have life, and have it to the full."* The devil constantly releases sickness, disease, turmoil, death and havoc while stirring up hatred. But Jesus came to bring life...fullness of life. Those who do not have a healthy body do *not* possess the fullness of life. Even if your toe throbs with chronic pain, it affects all of your body. If your head throbs with pain, you may not be able to function in day-to-day tasks. Nothing is too small for the Lord. If it steals life from you, Jesus is the answer.

Jesus came to destroy that which seeks to destroy you! Colossians 2:15 says, *"And having disarmed the powers and authorities, he made a public spectacle of them, triumphing over them by the cross."* Not only did Jesus come to give life, He completely defeated the enemy when He died on the cross. I often say that the enemy has been defeated...he has no feet. The enemy has been disarmed...he has no arms. The only thing he has left is a big mouth! Satan is called "the accuser of the brethren." Regardless, Jesus took care of that as well. Revelation 12:10-11, *Then I heard a loud voice in heaven say: "Now have come the salvation and the power and the kingdom of our God, and the authority of his Christ. For the accuser of our brothers, who accuses them before our God day and night, has been hurled down. They overcame him by the blood of the Lamb and by the word of their testimony; they did not love their lives so much as to shrink from death."*

We must stand in our authority and no longer allow the enemy to steal what rightfully belongs to us. The earth has been given to the children of God. You may think, "I can't do what Jesus did. I can't walk in the power that Samson did." Yes you can. Why, because His Spirit lives in you. Romans 8:11 says, *And if the Spirit of him who raised Jesus from the dead is living in you, he who raised Christ from the dead will also give life to your mortal bodies through his Spirit, who lives in you.*

Because Jesus' Spirit is in you, you have every bit of power and wisdom you need for life and godliness. 2 Peter 1:3 says, *"His divine power has given us everything we need for life and godliness through our knowledge of him who called us by his own glory and goodness."* You cannot say that you don't have what it takes to heal the sick or raise the dead. The Spirit of God lives in you! You have everything you need for life and the release of life in every form. "I can't do this, only Christ can." I am glad you said that. Philippians 4:13 says, *"I can do everything through him who gives me strength."*

If you truly believe the Word of God, your thinking must become: *I can do anything that is needed in every situation. Whatever opposition comes my way, I have what it takes to overcome.* If you really believe what the Word says, then nothing will be impossible for you. Galatians 2:20 says, *I have been crucified with Christ and I no longer live, but Christ lives in me. The life I live in the body, I live by faith in the Son of God, who loved me and gave himself for me.* This verse is NOT meant to be taken figuratively.

Too many people think, "Well, I realize that technically Christ lives in me but, really, I am a poor little powerless worm unable to do anything for God." Nonsense! You are powerful! The Spirit of God lives in you. You can do all things because it is no longer you living, but Christ living in you. When you look into my eyes you should no longer see Keith, you should see Christ.

I am Superman. I can fly!

I am faster than a speeding bullet; more powerful than a locomotive; able to leap tall buildings in a single bound. There is nothing prideful in declaring this. This is perfect humility. Jesus said we would do what He is doing and even *greater things*. John 14:12 (NLT) *"I tell you the truth, anyone who has faith in me will do what I have been doing. He will do even greater things than these, because I am going to the Father."* We are required by God to do what He says we can do...the impossible. We have received the promised Holy Spirit, who has empowered us to be His witnesses.

Acts 1:8 says, *But you will receive power when the Holy Spirit comes on you; and you will be my witnesses in Jerusalem, and in all Judea and Samaria, and to the ends of the earth.* Being a witness is not about waging an intellectual argument or apologetic as to why others need Jesus. Being a witness isn't about the four spiritual laws, the Romans Road, or any other evangelistic contrivance of well-meaning Christian leaders. Being a witness means bringing the power of Jesus into every situation that confronts you so that others will cry out, "We must have this Jesus you serve!" 1 Cor. 2:1-5 says, *When I came to you, brothers, I did not come with eloquence or superior wisdom as I proclaimed to you the testimony about God. For I resolved to know nothing while I was with you except Jesus Christ and him crucified. I came to you in weakness and fear, and with much trembling. My message and my preaching were not with wise and persuasive words, but with a demonstration of the Spirit's power, so that your faith might not rest on men's wisdom, but on God's power.*

To truly testify about the resurrected Lord requires releasing the power of resurrection life within you. The fullness of God's power lives in you. The only restriction is a lack of understanding of how to release what currently aches to break free. Therefore, if this power is not released, the deficiency comes from us...not God. We must learn how to respond to the nudges of the Spirit of God in everyday life if we desire to see the Spirit of His might and counsel coursing through our bodies. You are called to walk supernaturally because the supernatural One lives inside of you.

In the next chapter I would like to explore how God allows us to be a vessel that moves in heaven's reality, no matter what challenges are presented. We are called to be ones who bring the goodness of God into every situation we face. We are *not* at the mercy of the world's system because we do not serve the god of this world. The King of all Kings lives in us and will cause us to triumph in every situation no matter how dishonoring or disagreeable others are.

Chapter 10

Good Things Do Happen
at the Homefront

If we want to see the people of this world desire the reality of heaven in their lives, they must be drawn to us. Matthew 5:16 says, "...let your light shine before men, that they may see your good deeds and praise your Father in heaven." That light is Christ. If we do not hinder its visibility, others will draw near to this light. As the world becomes darker and darker those who are yielded to Him will become more and more attractive to the lost. Just as lighthouses once provided a beacon of hope to weary sea travelers, we too must be brilliant lights inviting those who are far off to draw near and encounter the fullness of God. People do not just need good theology, they need an encounter with God and we are the ones God has chosen to bring that encounter.

Rather than simply looking for signs and wonders, *be* the "sign and wonder." Interact. Engage. Immerse yourself in the lives of those around you. This is quite a contrast to the belief system of my early years, which seemed designed to keep us far away from the world we were called to reach. After all, unsaved people were evil sinners and if you got too close, they'd infect and contaminate you. I'm being a bit facetious, but in reality we stayed away from anything that "worldly" people did. Our job as Christians was to remain spotless until Jesus whisked us out of this "God-forsaken planet!" Daily, I checked my inner emotions, thoughts and outward actions to ensure I had not become tainted. The world and its sin were more powerful than the gospel hidden within me. Believers were encouraged to evangelize, but more from the perspective of convincing others to leave a lifestyle of sin and death rather than to experience God's loving-kindness and His power to touch every situation they might face.

We have to come to the place where we embrace the diversity we have as individuals and celebrate the unique characteristics found in us through Christ. You cannot be a "sign and a wonder" *and* focus on being disconnected from the world. The whole "be in the world but not of it" thing created a dysfunction in me wherein I was afraid to be *in* the world while at the same time terrified of rejection *from* the world. I had come to understand that being "different" from the world wasn't necessarily about being connected to an authentic self, but about my ability to remain outside of the world's influence. For example, "worldly" people went to movies, drank alcohol, had fun and dressed differently than believers. Our belief system held that by not participating in worldly things we would be shining lights, which would cause the world to somehow realize that our strikingly different behaviors were something they must have and eventually venture into the church to see about this Jesus we professed.

Truthfully, *this* Jesus was not nearly as attractive as the actual Jesus that walked the earth in first century Palestine. Somehow the authentic Jesus was able to eat and drink with sinners, hang out with them, receive their praise, extend forgiveness to those caught in sin...all the while staying free from the bondage of their struggles. Hebrews 2:18 says, *"Because he himself suffered when he was tempted, he is able to help those who are being tempted."* How was Jesus able to stay relevant and connected to the lost and hurting while also remaining clean and free of their sins? It is because He wasn't confused about His identity. Jesus knew how to be Himself in every situation. It was this authenticity that caused others to desire His company, attention, teaching and wisdom. His integrity was possible because He stayed in communion *with* and connected *to* His Heavenly Father. Luke 5:16 says, *"But Jesus often withdrew to lonely places and prayed."*

The "separatist" teaching caused me to stay as far away from unbelievers as possible and cultivated a fear that the world possessed more power than God—a fear that the devil was bigger than Christ in me. So deeply entrenched was this mentality that I carried it with me into pastoring. Breaking this powerless mentality wasn't easy. Allow me to share how the Lord set me free of that crippling, immobilizing mindset.

Keep in mind that Heather and I were twenty-two when we started pastoring and sometimes people who visited our church remarked, "Why, you're nothing more than snot-nosed kids. You're as young as my own kids," or something along those lines. One gentleman moved to Willits because the Lord had specifically told him to attend our church, but even he eventually shared similar sentiments with us about our young age and, not surprisingly, he was gone soon thereafter. Being young was challenging, as was stepping into something totally new for our church and region, while facing naysayers who presumed our youth made us unwise. But in spite of it all, we decided that no matter what people said, we would not be hindered from moving ahead into the *more* of God.

I know we unintentionally made many mistakes over the years. However, in Kingdom life whether what we do is messy or even erroneous, God actually applauds our effort and the faith it requires. Many times I have heard a loving Dad say, "Good job, son. Get up and dust yourself off after that fall. Try, try again and you will get it eventually." Proverbs 24:16 says, *"For though a righteous man falls seven times, he rises again, but the wicked are brought down by calamity. "*

Heather and I had attended a conference at Bethel Church in Redding, California, where we witnessed many signs and wonders. Faith seemed to invade every situation and the power of God flowed easily. But that was there, and we were now back home. And "home" was where nothing ever happened. At least that was the lie I had battled for years. And when we returned from the conference, that lie was blaring in my spirit: *No miracles happen in your hometown. You are without honor here.* On and on it went.

Once, I asked Bill Johnson, "How do you handle ministry in your hometown?" He responded, "When you have learned to minister without honor, then you can handle a ministry *with* honor." A powerful statement, but I had yet to learn that there were tremendous benefits to ministering in a place where people knew you well, such as the church I had grown up in and where I now pastored.

The enemy will say anything to restrain us from moving in the power of God that will change our environment. One day while thinking about these concepts, I took my children to a local store. Outside the store stood a child's bouncy house. We stopped and I let them jump in. While the kids jumped wildly inside the blow up structure, two women approached us. One of the ladies was on crutches and as they were passing by, I inquired about her legs. She informed me that she had Lyme's Disease and that sometimes her legs would simply give out, so I asked if I could pray for her. She agreed and I prayed.

At first, nothing happened. Her friend shook her head and remarked, "I'm done with this!" before turning and storming into the store. I asked the woman if I could pray again; again she agreed. After praying a second time she said that she felt a little better. When I prayed a third time she suddenly picked up her crutches, walked to her car and back telling me she was completely healed. I went home that day chanting, "Lyme's disease you got to go, you got to go, Lyme's disease you got to go." Incidentally, I saw this same woman a few months later and she said the only symptom remaining from the Lyme's disease was a bit of residual pain. She also said that she had a twin sister and when she had called to tell her about the healing, her twin's shoulder was healed as well.

Wow! Pretty amazing.

And...it happened in my hometown.

I was always more interested in advancing the Kingdom in my own town than in building my church, believing that if I advanced the Kingdom and did the things Jesus asked, then He would build the church as He promised. As a result, whenever I was out and about in the city, I wouldn't even tell the people I'd meet that I was a pastor.

One Sunday I sensed an extraordinary level of anointing flowing through my spirit; so much so that I went out on the streets after church. I saw a man with a cane walking along and with a holy boldness I approached him, inquired about his use of the cane and asked if I could pray for him. He told me that an accident twenty years earlier had left him with a bad back and he'd been out of work for many years. So, I prayed for him and as I did, his whole back began to audibly crack.

He stood up straight and walked around, still with the use of his cane. I said, "Give me your cane, you are healed!" and took the cane from him. He walked around without the cane, completely healed. His conclusion was that positive thinking had accomplished this for him. I replied, "No, this was Jesus. If it were positive thinking, it would have happened years ago." I walked with him the mile or so back to the trailer where he lived and told him that I wasn't going to allow him to keep his cane. The whole time I was with him, I didn't reveal to him that I was a pastor, or from a church, or anything of that nature. I didn't even tell him about his need for Jesus. I merely delivered the mail of God's goodness through the gift of healing.

A week later I found a sticky note on the door of our house, which at the time was adjacent to the church. It said, "I will see you in church on Sunday. Thanks Keith." I hadn't told him my name, but someone who knew me saw me praying for him and had told him who I was. He came to church with a Bible, which he had obtained from his psychiatrist. He went to the police station, turned in his medical marijuana card and eventually landed a job. He had pursued all of these things on his own without any prompting from me, all because this man had encountered the love of God...in my hometown!

As inspiring as these accounts are, we also faced some very challenging situations. Remember the couple in the park that I had prophesied over in order to break fear off my life? Months later they attended our church after she had been diagnosed with terminal cancer and the doctors had given her no hope to live. Apparently, she told her husband, "We must find the church where the young man who prayed for us attends. We need to go to a healing church." We had been called many things, but, "A healing church?" I was really excited to hear that.

By this time we had observed cancer healed several times and under some very interesting circumstances. One person healed from cancer was an elderly woman who lived right across the street from our home. She never attended church, but one afternoon when we were both in our front yards she hollered that she was going to have surgery for cancer. I immediately crossed the street and prayed for her. She said it was like lightning bolts of power were rushing through her body. After a subsequent examination her doctors declared her their cancer free "miracle lady."

As a result of these and other miracles, when the couple from the park arrived, even though the doctors had given the woman only a few weeks to live she held on to the hope that God would heal her and based on our success, we too were hopefully expectant.

Many people prayed and declared over her for weeks. Although she only seemed to get worse, she continued to come to our church and even formed friendships with several members of the congregation. Eventually, she became fully bed-ridden and at one point while visiting her in her home, she informed me that many of her friends had started to drop by to pay their last respects. I knew that we needed to surround her in love, or the constant flow of good-byes and farewells would cause her to lose hope.

Nurses came and went doing what they could to prepare both husband and wife for the eventuality of her death. I, however, still had faith that she could be healed. As I talked with her of God's goodness she revived and stood up, walking around the room while excitedly talking with me about the goodness of God.

One day her husband called me and said, "Keith, I can't allow you to continue seeing my wife. The false hope you give her is the only thing keeping her alive. You need to tell her to let go so she can die."

He had stood by her through her pain and suffering for a very long time. While I understood that, I've got to be honest—this produced a profound struggle within my spirit: How could I tell her to give up on the very thing I had fought so hard to see established? I finally called Kris Vallotton to ask for wisdom. He said, "You can't do that Keith. One day you will write about this story and you have to hold on to what you are fighting to establish."

So I called the husband back and told him I that I couldn't quit— that I had to keep praying. He replied, "Well, then, you aren't allowed to visit and you cannot talk to her anymore."

I am sad to say that within a couple of days...she died.

The whole ordeal crushed me. Even worse was the fact that because of my relentless pursuit of her healing, the husband considered me to be an evil influence and attempted to stir up trouble within our church body. He even stood outside the church one day with signs to that effect. I would be less than honest if I didn't confess that it was profoundly upsetting. But, he was in terrible emotional pain and, as a result, I couldn't really blame him for the actions his grief prompted him to take.

I share this story to say that not every experience in my hometown was easy. Stories travel quickly in small towns and sometimes the ones closest to you—the people with whom you have journeyed—side with those who don't speak the truth and people get pulled away. It is all a part of learning how to continue to love and honor...even when it isn't reciprocated.

I have since moved on from my hometown, but I still return from time to time and continue to build relationship with the church there. They have a high level of honor for me...and I for them. The Lord is building the church in Willits and it is by His grace that it is being built. What was once a place of dishonor for me, ultimately became a place of honor.

One thing I love about Jesus is that He refused to be a victim of His circumstances. He didn't tiptoe around any situation, but remained true to who He was, connected to the Father and able to relate to diverse people in diverse situations. Even when He was without honor, disliked, hated, persecuted, misunderstood and betrayed by

His own disciples, He courageously held His course...and so must we. The world is hungry for what we have—a phenomenal, life-giving relationship with God. Anybody who truly encounters Him will never desire to go back. John 3:16 says, *"For God so loved the world that he gave his one and only Son, that whoever believes in him shall not perish but have eternal life."* There is incredible life available to all who will seek—the secret formula to the fountain of youth; a well of unending happiness and peace that is greater than any negative circumstance the world can throw against us.

There is a massive harvest ready to be gathered and truly the fields are ripe, but, as the Bible says, the workers are few. This is not due to a lack of Christians in the world, for there are many who profess the name of Christ, but because many of the workers hide behind walls of fear, insecurity and lack of revelation of the great power in them. In short, the spirit of antichrist is alive and well.

What is this "antichrist" spirit? Christ means, "Anointed King." Therefore, antichrist means, "anti-anointing or anti-King." The antichrist spirit stands in direct contention against the Holy Spirit of God moving freely in our midst *and* in the world. The world doesn't just need good theology and moral character lessons; it needs a good dose of Holy Spirit joy, hope, healing, prophecy and love. What the world needs is Christ in you.

The only thing that can hold back this great harvest is you remaining sheltered within the comfort of the church building, hidden in constant meetings and endless teachings. I will reiterate: The enemy does not care if you have a little fire as long as you keep it in the "fireplace" of the church or your private life.

You are not called to keep the good news of Jesus quiet. I'm pretty sure that if your favorite food were going to be given away at your favorite restaurant on a particular day of the month, you wouldn't keep it a secret, but would tell everyone about it. People who keep the power of the Holy Spirit hidden in their lives just haven't experienced its effect to the extent that it provokes them to move outside of their comfort zones. In order to get the good news of His power and His solutions to a world in desperate need, you have to overcome your own feelings of inadequacy. Many men and woman, both in the Bible and throughout church history, had to rise above fear, insecurity and feelings of inadequacy in order to be who they were meant to be.

Exodus 4:1 says, *"Moses answered, "What if they do not believe me or listen to me and say, 'The Lord did not appear to you'?"* Not only did Moses struggle with whether or not he would be received, he argued with God about his ability to speak God's word. Exodus 4:10, *"Moses said to the Lord, "O Lord, I have never been eloquent, neither in the past nor since you have spoken to your servant. I am slow of speech and tongue."* Notice God's response to his sense of inadequacy. Exodus 4:11-14, *The Lord said to him, "Who gave man his mouth? Who makes him deaf or mute? Who gives him sight or makes him blind? Is it not I, the LORD? Now go; I will help you speak and will teach you what to say." But Moses said, "O Lord, please send someone else to do it." Then the Lord's anger burned against Moses...*

God is looking for someone that will say with confidence, *"What, then, shall we say in response to this? If God is for us, who can be against us?"* (Romans 8:31) And, *"I can do everything through him who gives me strength."* (Philippians 4:13)

We cannot ask God to send laborers into the field without the willingness to go ourselves. Prayers for the harvest—for God to send laborers into the field—cannot be directed toward someone else. You must become a father and mother to what you birth in prayer. In Matthew 9:37-38 Jesus asks His disciples to pray. *"Then he said to his disciples, "The harvest is plentiful but the workers are few. Ask the Lord of the harvest, therefore, to send out workers into his harvest field."* Notice the very next verse where Jesus called His disciples to Himself and gave them authority to go out as workers. Matthew 10:1, He *called his twelve disciples to him and gave them authority to drive out evil spirits and to heal every disease and sickness.* The areas for which you passionately pray are the very areas in which you may be called to become an answer.

Once, while traveling to minister in another church, the Lord asked, "Keith, are you going to father what you birth today in this service?" That really set me to thinking deeply. *Do I take these ministry times lightly? Oh, I'll pray into something, be a part of ministering there, but do I care enough to continue to stay with them in the journey?* I responded, "Yes, Lord I will father what is birthed in the spirit."

The answer to the question the Lord asks each one of us must be, "Yes, Lord I will go and be a part of the answer to the prayers that are being prayed." It is one thing to pray during meetings where we feel provoked, excited and in a place of intimacy with God; or during a great worship service when we are singing at the top of our lungs, "Anywhere You want me to go I will go. Anything You want me to do I will do. I say yes to You Lord." It's another thing altogether, however, when God puts a need right in front of us and we claim, "I am not qualified. I do not have the time. I do not have the training. They won't receive me." We cannot say those things and expect the Lord to continually bless our prayers.

David provides another excellent example. He was unwilling to make a sacrifice to God that cost him nothing. 2 Samuel 24:24, *But the king replied to Araunah, "No, I insist on paying you for it. I will not sacrifice to the LORD my God burnt offerings that cost me nothing." So David bought the threshing floor and the oxen and paid fifty shekels of silver for them.* In order for fire to fall there has to be sacrifice; there has to be willingness. Many people believe they are too old, too young, have made too many mistakes, or their past is too riddled with sin. It is time to stop the excuses — stop being a victim of your circumstances. Luke 1:37 says, *"For nothing is impossible with God."*

Are you going to be the one remembered in the extended version of Hebrews 11 as a person of faith, or as one who buried their talents in the sand? Hosea overcame being married to a prostitute; Moses was a murderer with an anger problem; Peter constantly put his foot in his mouth; and Paul was a mass murderer completely against the move of God. Hebrews 11:32-39 says, *And what more shall I say? I do not have time to tell about Gideon, Barak, Samson, Jephthah, David, Samuel and the* prophets, *who through faith conquered kingdoms, administered justice, and gained what was promised; who shut the mouths of lions, quenched the fury of the flames, and escaped the edge of the sword; whose weakness was turned to strength; and who became powerful in battle and routed foreign armies. Women received back their dead, raised to life again. Others were tortured and refused to be released, so that they might gain a better resurrection. Some faced jeers and flogging, while still others were chained and put in prison. They were stoned; they were sawed in two; they were put to death by the sword. They went about in sheepskins and goatskins, destitute, persecuted and mistreated – the world was not worthy of them. They wandered in deserts and mountains, and in caves and holes in the ground. These were all commended for their faith..."*

Put your name at the end of this passage and write in what you are going to be known for. I would write, *Keith was a man completely against this move of God; joyless, powerless, religious; a man who struggled to receive God's love; a man rejected by his own church network, but who rose up to become a world changer, a heavenly Kingdom bringer, a carrier of joy and one easily receptive to God's love. Keith is a man who has large arms of love to embrace many.*

Write out your own Hebrews 11 declaration. What will be written on your tombstone? He was a good man? Or that *He was a fiery-full-of-the-Holy Spirit-trailblazing-fearless-envelope pushing-distributor-of-the-Kingdom on this earth revolutionary, who helped us see that there was more.* I believe you have what it takes to overcome every adversity in your life and become a mighty force to be reckoned with. You have been born at exactly the right time. You can no longer despise your age, your background, your physical appearance or lack of qualifications. God has chosen you! Will you say yes to what He has birthed in your spirit through prayer and change your world? I believe you will say, "Yes!" and see your world changed for the glory of God.

Once you have said "Yes!" you must not allow anything to hinder the purpose of your life. You are on your way to becoming a conquering warrior. Conquering warriors are those who break through resistance into the promised lands that await them. Once you have learned how to victoriously navigate your way through opposition, lack of honor and persecution you are ready to handle the Promised Land.

In the next chapter we will pursue being intentional about expanding the Kingdom of God and walking out personal promises you have received from Him.

Chapter 11

The Spirit of Breakthrough

In order to see the kingdoms of this world transformed into the Kingdoms of our God, we first need a spirit of breakthrough. One revelation Heather and I learned during this season of entering into the *more* of God was this: If you push long enough you will eventually see the fulfillment of the promises you believe. There is a spirit of acceleration present in this season acting as the catalyst to fulfill promises at an increased rate. As we stepped into our identity as overcomers we had to learn how to fight through many things.

I had the enduring belief that if I stayed in motion long enough I would eventually see my desires become reality. However, the church organization of my childhood did not foster the attitude of being a godly overcomer. Instead, we were fed a constant diet of, "The world is getting stronger, the darkness is getting darker, and the devil is getting bigger" — a mindset that produces a sense of hopelessness.

In my younger years, I remember seeing many people cloaked in discouragement, never stepping into their identities or living up to their potential; living predictable lives that required little or no risk and little or no courage. As a result, fear caused many to never pursue their dreams and the lack of a relational culture fed into this fear. To truly believe that *there must be more* requires a spirit of breakthrough, the same spirit required to walk out of the land of predictable living into the land of new adventure. Stepping into that land was like dipping my toes into cold water, a difficult and slow process. But once I tasted the new fruit...I was hooked! I knew there was more and if I pushed long enough I would reach it.

Establishing a supernatural culture, confronting fear, overcoming enemies and learning to live relationally, required a spirit of breakthrough. Possessing things in the Spirit requires more than a dreamy thought...it requires an unshakable resolve! I believe God blessed me with the spirit of a fighter—a spirit that simply will not quit. In fact, my name Keith, means, "one meant for the battlefield." Deep within my soul I have always known that if I push long enough I will eventually obtain that for which I battle.

There are three vital components to manifestation of the reality you desire and battle for on the front lines. The first component is perseverance; the second, breakthrough; the third is follow-through. Allow me to share a story encompassing these three components.

The Lord gave me a promise one day that I was pregnant with potential. He said, "Keith, you may have whatever house you want." Since I had spent the majority of my life living in parsonages—homes adjacent to a church building where the pastor and his family reside—this was a difficult concept for me to grasp. Mainly because somewhere in the culture of my upbringing was the unspoken belief that pastors should never own or retain anything of value for themselves. Being poor was the goal and a sign of *true* spirituality. Let me just go ahead and tell you that being poor is highly overrated! But that's a story for another time.

When I received the promise, I did not understand how the Spirit of breakthrough operated. I assumed that if the Lord promised you something, it would come to pass and that was that. But I knew that I had heard the voice of God, so I truly knew this promise was an assurance from the Lord and not something I had fashioned myself. I shared the word with Heather and it resonated in both of our spirits. We had lived in a parsonage for about seven years of our married life. The home was in dire need of repair and, in fact, contained mold, which contributed to many physical problems Heather was experiencing. It was time to leave that place behind. However, there were many things I would have to overcome internally in order to handle homeownership.

When we began our search for a new house, we walked through some fine homes located in an area called Brooktrails. It was a beautiful area in pine and redwood forests, filled with peaceful streams; deer, turkey and other stunning parts of creation. We eventually found a lovely house and even though at the time had no concept of how it would become ours, we moved forward in the buying process knowing that God told us we could have whatever house we wanted.

Heather and I met the owners and told them we were very excited about making this house our own. They asked whether we had secured a loan and we assured them that we were certain all the financial matters would work out. We returned several times to walk through the house and dream about it becoming ours. The truth is, we were very naïve regarding virtually every aspect of the buying process. But, we had a promise from the Lord and actually believed that God would fulfill His Word even going so far as to assume the owners would merely sign the papers over to us as a sovereign act of God blessing us with a fully paid piece of property.

One afternoon as we drove by our "promised land" we noticed a "Sold" sign on the house. The terms "stunned, surprise and devastation" come nowhere near to describing our feelings. There was no way this house could belong to anyone but us! We investigated further and discovered that it had, indeed, been sold to someone who actually possessed the finances to purchase it. Imagine that. What a shock this was to our innocent understanding of how God works. We spent the following week discouraged and perplexed. For both of us, it seemed that the presence of God was far away. I began to question whether or not I had even heard from the Lord. Did He really say I could have whatever house I wanted, or had I completely missed it? Having assumed that since I had a promise I would most certainly see it fulfilled in the first place I set my plow, I simply didn't understand how it would now unfold.

After a week of battling bewilderment we found hope again. While listening to a message by Bill Johnson we were struck by his statement that, "If you step into unbelief toward God's promises, you need to repent and step back into believing Him." We recognized our unbelief and repented by saying, "God, we believe what you said is true." While it was true that God wanted to give us this house, we needed to make room for the possibility that perhaps there was a process we had to undergo in order to be ready to steward the gift.

After this experience Heather and I actively searched for financing. Beyond an occasional car loan, where most times we had simply signed on the dotted line, I was completely unfamiliar with the process. We learned that while we could indeed qualify for a loan, based on our income we could only afford a "fixer upper." Thus, we began a new search for a house more suited to our financial means. We viewed many houses and actually found a few we liked. The idea of having a fixer upper was something we could live with. We spent a considerable amount of time dreaming about the specific kind of house we wanted including what kind of street we would love to call home and even the various features we'd like to see both inside and outside. We envisioned a pool, hot tub, prayer room, and nice view — somewhere we could host loved ones and visitors alike. Through it all we began to understand the process of the promise.

At one point I remember thinking to myself, *The Lord did not tell us we could only have a fixer upper. He said we could have whatever house we wanted.* I informed Heather that I wanted to continue looking for the kind of houses we desired in our hearts and that I didn't care about the cost. I wanted a house with all the features we had discussed and dreamed about. Up to that point, we had only been looking at houses within our price range, but from that moment forward, we purposely redirected our search toward finding the house we truly desired.

And find it we did.

It was even on one of the streets we liked. It had our checklist of features: pool, hot tub, prayer room, great location, quiet neighborhood, and room to host guests. It was our dream home. The only problem was that it cost twice as much as we could afford.

We didn't know how to proceed, so we simply waited...and waited... and waited some more. And then a little more. After a few more weeks had passed we finally felt the time had come to step out in faith, so we decided to make an offer, knowing full well that once the offer was made—and a full-price offer at that—we'd be legally responsible to produce the appropriate finances. There was quietness in the Spirit and neither of us had the slightest sense of the Lord speaking during this time. The only thing we knew for certain was that He had spoken and we had to respond in faith while at the same time remaining watchful to see His plan unfold.

Then something amazing happened. As soon as we made the offer some money unexpectedly arrived. Our church discovered that there was a portion of our salary that had inadvertently been withheld over a seven-year period. Miraculously, there were now sufficient funds in the account to cover all of the back pay. We also managed to procure a loan that was structured in such a way that it offered us greater financial ability. Even though the battle to acquire the house was at times intense, it eventually became ours...the impossible became a reality.

This was a pivotal achievement, for we had never before owned a home. In the weeks following I wrestled with many complex thoughts and emotions, mainly because this house was incredible—even nicer than many of our church members' homes. "What will they think of me owning something so nice?" and other doubtful, fearful thoughts raced through my mind. On moving day I listened to a sermon by Kim Clement. He said, "When the Lord gives you a promise and you fully walk into it, your path brings breakthrough—not only for you but also for many others. If you do not receive your blessing then others cannot receive theirs."

We moved into a house that, based on our earnings, was twice the amount we could afford. It was not a "fixer upper," but a custom built home with a bedroom for each of our children as well as a separate bedroom for guests. We also had a private prayer room where we stored our instruments, art equipment and even a rocking chair to soak in the presence of the Lord. Heather and I spent many hours in those "prophet's chambers." Our family, as well as our guests, enjoyed that pool, hot tub and large deck to the fullest over the next several years. What God had promised more than a year before, He accomplished. I remember gazing at the large boulders that lined our front driveway and thinking, *God, You are faithful. That is who You are. You are that Rock. You are faithful, who spoke a word into my spirit and brought it to fruition.*

True to what Kim Clement taught, within a matter of months following our breakthrough three or four members of our congregation who had been unable to own a home purchased new homes. Once we had broken through in this promise, a passage was torn open in the Spirit; a resistant wall shattered and others were now enjoying the benefits of our promise. Your fulfilled promises become testimonies prophesying to others: "If God did it for me, He can do it for you."

Many people in the early days of American history pioneered new lands, fought battles and carved out paths to the uncharted territories of our great nation so that others could follow. In the same way, we hack and cut through the brush of spiritual resistance forging new trails for the benefit of those who come after. Those who follow then walk a path already carved out for them and our testimony supplies them with courage and the assurance that breakthrough is just on the other side.

Once you have broken through, it is important that you persevere until breakthrough is established. We experienced unexpected financial favor that allowed us to purchase a house that was worth more than we could afford. However, now that we were in the house we wanted to be able to eat more than ramen noodle soup every day, so we knew we had to grow into this promise that had been granted us. For the first year our salary, as generous as it was, was not enough to sustain our new situation. Then, after a year our adjustable rate mortgage changed increasing our payment eight hundred dollars per month. As a result, we were slowly being eaten alive! We explored loan options with other home lenders but were unable to find a better loan.

Right about that time I attended a meeting to connect with other friends in ministry and was asked to facilitate the offering. I was in no condition to take the offering! I was discouraged, hopeless and feeling nothing like a mighty man of faith. I said to myself, "How am I going to encourage people to give anything in my emotional state?" I sensed the Lord saying, "Just share testimonies of my faithfulness from your past." So, I shared stories of how God had provided for us financially and how He could do it for anyone, at any moment. I did not feel anything significant in my spirit as I spoke; no wonderful feeling of excitement...nothing! It was simply an act of obedience to share God's testimony.

When I returned home that evening an email sat in my inbox from one of our loan agents. It read, "Great news, Keith. I found a fixed rate loan that will solve your financial issues and get you back on the right track with this house." She went on to say that she had personally used this loan and that it was just what we needed. Praise the Lord! After I had shared the testimonies of God's faithfulness He proved Himself faithful again. Such wonder, such awe we had for Him.

Our loan was now at a rate more suited to our income, but we were still in a very tight spot financially. Something else had to change to shift our finances. Heather had been urged by the Lord to do some work with the children of our city and eventually found herself heading up the after-school program in one of our local schools. She carried tremendous favor. The Lord opened many doors for her to bless the children of our city and also work with key leaders in the community. That job became a huge blessing and within a year helped to stabilize our finances. Not only was there enough to cover our basic needs but also enough left over to set aside monthly savings. We finally began to enjoy our lifestyle. The promise spoken four years beforehand required one year for initial breakthrough and three years to become fully established.

When God speaks, you will find that hidden in His word is every bit of wisdom, every bit of hope and every bit of faith you need to navigate through opposition and to keep you moving in the right direction.

Hidden in the vision of His word is the provision to see it become a reality. Nothing can stand in the way of the Word of the Lord if you keep your heart wrapped around what He has said. Did Heather and I undergo this process perfectly? No. We made fundamental mistakes, like not consulting our mentors until after we had acquired the house. Perhaps their wisdom could have helped us avoid hardships. Despite the challenges, or even ignorance in this matter, God was faithful to teach us how to attain breakthrough and establish the promise He had given.

It is possible that the Lord has presented you with a promise that has yet to come to pass. If so, this much is certain: You absolutely must release your idea of how it will be fulfilled. We had no idea His promise meant that our first "dream house" would not be ours...nor would the second or the third. The Lord intended all along to guide us through a very specific and intentional process. Lacking the financial wherewithal to bring the promise to fulfillment on our own, we had to learn how to lean on Him. He showed us how to live in our "promised land" and expand our financial base in order to enjoy His gift, His promise. Every area in life where you desire breakthrough will involve this kind of process. It will not happen merely because He has made a promise. You must seize His word and never let go.

1 Timothy 1:18-19 says, *Timothy, my son, I give you this instruction in keeping with the prophecies once made about you, so that by following them you may fight the good fight, holding on to faith and a good conscience. Some have rejected these and so have shipwrecked their faith.* If you yearn to see the Lord's promises and prophetic declarations become a reality, you must hold onto them with steadfastness, tenacity, boldness and courage. Hopelessness likes to creep in, especially if the promise has been slow to arrive. Proverbs 13:12 says, *"Hope deferred makes the heart sick, but a longing fulfilled is a tree of life."* Hopelessness does, indeed, make your heart sick and can cause you to lose the sense of His presence and honesty compels me to confess that there were several times during this process when Heather and I lost hope. Some of the most challenging moments in life come as a result of allowing our hearts to

be overwhelmed by a seemingly impossible situation.

Zachariah, the father of John the Baptist, was given a promise that couldn't be understood within the context of his reality He was an old man and his wife too was well along in years. He resorted to unbelief instead of simple trust in God's Word; thus, he was struck silent for a period of time. Luke 1:19-20 says, *The angel answered, "I am Gabriel. I stand in the presence of God, and I have been sent to speak to you and to tell you this good news. And now you will be silent and not able to speak until the day this happens, because you did not believe my words, which will come true at their proper time.* God was so good that even though Zachariah did not believe, the promise still came to fruition, albeit at tremendous cost to Zechariah.

On the other hand, Mary, the mother of Jesus, had a similar promise given to her. She was told that as a virgin she would bear a child, the Son of God, which, in my opinion, was at least *as* hard if not harder to believe than the promise God presented to Zachariah. But instead of wondering how this word would take place, Mary responded with "yes." Luke 1:35-38, *The angel answered, "The Holy Spirit will come upon you, and the power of the Most High will overshadow you. So the holy one to be born will be called the Son of God. Even Elizabeth your relative is going to have a child in her old age, and she who was said to be barren is in her sixth month. For nothing is impossible with God." "I am the Lord's servant, "Mary answered, "May it be to me as you have said." Then the angel left her.*

I love it! This young girl was truly a mighty woman of faith. Nothing is impossible with God. The TNIV version of Luke 1:37 says, *"For no word of God will ever fail."* He is so faithful to bring to pass that which He promises. Our hearts are not always meant to understand what He has said. God desires that we offer a resounding "Yes!" instead of wondering how the word will be accomplished. When we wrap our hearts around the impossibilities we find discouragement, hopelessness and despair. When we wrap our hearts around testimonies of God's faithfulness in our lives and the lives of others, we will gain endless hope. As I have heard it said by our senior leader, David Crone, "When you say yes to God...you receive hope." Saying yes during the journey is the key to seeing your promised land become a reality.

I'm sure you're familiar with the story of Gideon. The Lord declared him to be a mighty warrior and told him to go save Israel from the enemy. Judges 6:12-14, *"When the angel of the Lord appeared to Gideon, he said, "The Lord is with you, mighty warrior."* And verse 14, *"The Lord turned to him and said, "Go in the strength you have and save Israel out of Midian's hand. Am I not sending you?"* God declared Gideon's identity, and it was *that* declaration that provided the needed ingredients for him to become a mighty warrior that could lead an army into victory.

When God speaks a word into your own life, it is not just meant to lift your spirits or to make you feel better about yourself. As with Gideon, His word carries everything necessary for you to walk into your identity. Gideon had to wrestle with that word for some time, but God was patient and gracious as He always is. The Lord provided many signs to encourage Gideon along the way to becoming the man He had declared him to be: A victorious warrior.

Once you receive the promise you can take it to the area that requires breakthrough and sledge hammer your way through the resistance until that wall crumbles. Some of the walls that must disintegrate are internal walls of doubt that continually proclaim, "This is impossible!" Gideon had to wrestle with whether the word was true and, if so, where was God when he needed Him? Gideon was hopeless. Judges 6:13, *But sir," Gideon replied, "if the LORD is with us, why has all this happened to us? Where are all his wonders that our fathers told us about when they said, 'Did not the LORD bring us up out of Egypt?' But now the LORD has abandoned us and put us into the hand of Midian.*

I don't know about you, but this seems ironic to the point of being comical. Here was the Lord Himself speaking through an angel, and Gideon's response is, *"If the Lord is with us?"* Excuse me, but if I'm conversing with an angel, it seems like a pretty clear sign that the Lord *is* with me.

In order to take a promise off the bookshelf of our hearts and actually believe it, we must confront areas in our lives that claim, "Well, I tried this before and it did not work out too well." "I believed God and He didn't come through. " "Well, brother, you just don't know what I face every day or the obstacles I deal with." "You do not know how many times I have tried and failed!" As long as you focus on the failures of your life, the hopelessness of your circumstances, the status of your family, or the nation's economy, you will never step into your promised land. Promised lands are meant for warriors who believe God regardless of the opposition. The one who is in you can do all things. Philippians 4:13 says, *"I can do everything through him who gives me strength."* The Lord normally gives us our promised land in stages, which allows us to be strengthened little by little so that when we arrive in the Promised Land we can steward what we have received. Exodus 23:29-30 says, *But I will not drive them out in a single year, because the land would become desolate and the wild animals too numerous for you. Little by little I will drive them out before you, until you have increased enough to take possession of the land.* The Lord does not want to give us something too substantial so that when we receive it we won't have the strength, manpower, or finances to rule and subdue it. He doesn't want us overwhelmed and destroyed by His gift...He wants us to enjoy it.

Gideon did not immediately lead the army to victory. In fact, he first wrestled with his own insecurities. He asked God over and over again for a sign. Ultimately, Gideon had to confront his family idols. The Lord told him he had to take them down before he could pursue the enemy. Judges 6:25-27, *That same night the LORD said to him, "Take the second bull from your father's herd, the one seven years old. Tear down your father's altar to Baal and cut down the Asherah pole beside it. Then build a proper kind of altar to the Lord your God on the top of this height. Using the wood of the Asherah pole that you cut down, offer the second bull as a burnt offering. 'So Gideon took ten of his servants and did as the Lord told him. But because he was afraid of his family and the men of the town, he did it at night rather than in the daytime.*

Before you will be given the land of your enemies, you must first retrieve the land of your fathers in personal issues. This will strengthen you to handle the land the Lord wants to give you.

Regarding our house hunt, I had to wrestle with having always lived in a parsonage. *Would people think I squandered the church money so I could live lavishly?* On and on the thoughts raced until I broke through and finally understood my value and God's desire to bless me. I needed to understand that my blessings were not only significant to my own life and the life of my family, but were meant to open a door of blessing for others, thereby creating a ripple effect in the Kingdom. God's desire was for us to have the desires of our heart fulfilled and be a sign to those in our world that His word is true.

Gideon experienced breakthrough, destroyed his father's idols and ultimately rose up to become a man with sufficient resolve to muster an army of thirty-two thousand. The Lord whittled the army down to the three hundred who had said "Yes" in their heart to God's ability to bring victory. One man who has said yes, backed by three hundred others who have said yes, is an unshakable force.

Gideon obeyed the Lord's strategy, which resulted in sending the enemy army into confusion, fleeing for their lives. As the enemy began to retreat, Gideon and his men became extremely fatigued. Judges 8:4 says, *"Gideon and his three hundred men, exhausted yet keeping up the pursuit, came to the Jordan and crossed it."* They maintained pursuit until the enemy and their leaders were captured and killed. Judges 8:12, *"Zebah and Zalmunna, the two kings of Midian, fled, but he pursued them and captured them, routing their entire army."*

The key to establishing breakthrough is to remain steadfast until you have fully acquired the object of your pursuit. Attaining our house was not the fulfillment of the promise. Would God have given us a house that we could not enjoy because our finances did not allow it? No. We had to continue the pursuit of His promise until that promise had been fully established and the land was ours. It required an additional three years of holding on, pressing in through faith, combating hopelessness and believing His everlasting word.

Many people can break through in God. However, I am interested in breaking into *new* places in God and establishing those as "normal" in my life and the lives of others. Prophecy was once foreign to me, but has now become my normal. Miracles were once foreign, but are now expected. Once while in Fiji, I led a group out onto the streets to pray and minister to people. We saw a deaf woman's ear opened up, legs healed, people prophesied over and lives changed, all by a group of people who had learned just the week before that this power was available to them. When God's power and prophetic breakthrough has been established in lives, there is less danger of being taken over again by the enemy.

I do not want to fight for a promised land that I cannot hold, manage and expand. Many people who have seen the power of God eventually lose it because they don't continually share with others how to walk in it. The goal is to establish the promises of God in your life until you fully delight in the promise and then impart your breakthrough into others until they are established as well.

Although we are fighting to fully lay hold of all that God says is available, God has interesting turns in the road that occasionally seem to go against the previous promises. After our family had enjoyed our Promised Land and new house for three years we were invited to move to Vacaville to pursue other promised lands that were in our heart. In the process the land we had fought so hard for – our house, friends and church – had to be surrendered in order to go to another level. We retained our friendships and connection with our church but our house had to go.

We put our house up for sale during the time in our nation when the housing market crashed. As a result, we found no buyer. Even though we fought hard to see our house sold, there was no breakthrough. Eventually we heard a gentle whisper from the Lord saying, "Let the house go." So, we let the house go into foreclosure. While it seemed like a defeat at the time it was something we were willing to go through. Stepping into a greater dimension of our promised land required the sacrifice of promises fulfilled before. It was painful, yet joyous. It is not every day we get to offer God something that is dear to our hearts. There is no regret in this decision, as we know that whenever we give up houses for the sake of the Kingdom there will be an even greater return. Mark 10:29-30 says, *"I tell you the truth," Jesus replied, "no one who has left home or brothers or sisters or mother or father or children or fields for me and the gospel will fail to receive a hundred times as much in this present age (homes, brothers, sisters, mothers, children and fields – and with them, persecutions) and in the age to come, eternal life."*

What an exciting adventure. There are many wonderful promises of God and with every one of them He says, "Yes, my child, you can have that one." When we say "amen" to His "Yes!" we are on our way to seeing that promise become a reality. It takes courage, hope and resolve to step toward a promise that has yet to exist in your life, or the lives of others around you. It takes holding on and declaring life from the word of the Lord. It takes staying close to God so that when you break through you keep pursuing the promise until the breakthrough becomes a fortress built on the land you have acquired. You are not meant to live with unfulfilled promises...you are meant to live in your promised land!

I release courage to you today. If God could bring things that were once foreign to pass in my life, He can do the same for you. If I could enter into a lifestyle of the supernatural and a culture of healthy relationships when none of those were present in my life, then certainly nothing is impossible with God. If He can do it for me, He can do it for you. The sky is the limit and then...there is more. I say, "Yes!" Lord.

If we are to remain in the promised lands He gives us there are certain characteristics in our nature that need to be established. One of those characteristics is joy. Joy is the strength that keeps you moving toward a greater expression of God's Kingdom manifested in your life. In the next few chapters we will explore the process required to establish a lifestyle of joy – a necessity for all true pioneers.

Chapter 12

A Rabbit Hole to Hidden Wonders

A few years ago I told the Lord that I hungered for one thing from Him...joy. He proceeded to lead me down a "rabbit hole" of heavenly mysteries. It was a journey of discovering that joy is, in fact, a part of the atmosphere of heaven and the nature of God. This life-altering revelation, as liberating as it was, stood as a direct challenge to the belief system that had developed in me over the years of growing up in church.

In the Disney movie, *Pollyanna*, a young girl arrives in a town full of negative, grumpy people. She innocently transforms the heart of a community through playing the "glad game" and sharing her belief that God is in a good mood and is a God of blessing and encouragement. The point of the "glad game" is to find the treasure in everything and everyone. One of the more pointed scenes of the movie takes place when Pollyanna runs into a "hellfire and brimstone" preacher, Reverend Ford. His core message originates from the concept that God is easily angered, severe and humorless. This God concept affects the way he read scripture and views people. Then along comes Pollyanna. The day Reverend Ford met Pollyanna was the day he began to be captured by her contagious, positive way of viewing God. Ultimately, his entire life and ministry is transformed. If you'll allow me the analogy, I *was* Reverend Ford.

In my early years of church life I had come to believe that a spiritual person was a serious person because God was a serious and rather frightening being. This belief became a mindset and from that mindset I assumed that He was easily angered and rarely happy. I did not have a correct view of my Daddy God who fully loves and accepts me. Fear of failure kept me on the treadmill of guilt and condemnation where I became entrenched in heaviness, seriousness of thought and actions, as well as general discouragement, all of which robbed me of true joy. My concept of the Holy Spirit included the belief that He was constantly grieved by my thoughts and actions. I felt I had to tiptoe around hoping to keep Him happy. If I made a mistake, I'd better repent quickly or He would be angry and distant.

Then along came God. One day the Lord revealed to me a picture of the Holy Spirit as a person. He appeared in the form of one of my mentors laughing his head off. God revealed through this vision that the Holy Spirit is not easily grieved with me, but that He is lighthearted and much more fun than I could ever imagine. One of the passages that came alive to me is, *"For the Kingdom of God is not a matter of eating and drinking, but of righteousness, peace and joy in the Holy Spirit."* (Romans 14:17) This passage tells us that one of the characteristics of the Holy Spirit is joy. It is not just an occasional encounter. God is joy. It is who He is, not something He does once in a while.

Knowing that God did not just tolerate me, but that He is thrilled with me as His son has brought tremendous freedom. The renewing of my mind and living in this freedom has led me into many joy encounters. I had to not only change the way I viewed God, but also change the way I lived life. Allow me to share a little of my journey into experiencing the joy of heaven's culture.

Being uncertain of exactly how to go about acquiring joy in my life, I began with a daily routine of exercising laughter in my prayer closet as an attempt to "prime the pump." For weeks, I played a CD, which was a compilation of outbreaks of laughter in several different church meetings. In the beginning it did not feel like any water could be found in the parched desert of my heart. Those who happened to pass by my prayer closet later remarked that my laughter sounded fake and dry, but I didn't care! Something inside of me was intent on discovering joy. The Lord set me up. He wanted me to break out of a lifestyle of dry and serious Christianity and enter into a place of constant refreshment in Him.

One Friday evening, after months of "priming the pump," the Lord said, "I am now going to release this joy into your church. Have your brother Paul begin the Friday night service and I will release joy into the house." So I asked Paul to start the service however he felt led. Keep in mind that manifestations of joy were not customary in our church. Paul grabbed a large jug that we used for missions' offerings and started walking up and down the aisles of the sanctuary pouring imaginary water over people while instructing them to drink. Among our guests that evening was a regional pastor. Quickly, laughter erupted in the room. Some people fell uncontrollably onto the carpeted floor while others rolled around, frivolously laughing and colliding into one another.

I looked around at those immersed in laughter (to be honest something I thought rather foolish at the time) wondering how I could possibly restore order? I was asking myself, *Is this okay in the house of God? Some of these people are not even "spiritual!" They have issues to work on, Lord.* And the Lord stopped me, saying very clearly, "Keep your hands off this!" Although I enjoyed the initial waters of joy bursting forth, I struggled with the urge to control this new manifestation. The Lord has since led me through a process where I understand the importance of laughter and lightness. Proverbs 17:22 says, *"A cheerful heart is good medicine, but a crushed spirit dries up the bones."*

I've read that children laugh on average 400 times per day versus adults, who average 15 times per day. As we grow older, we tend to become encumbered by life's challenges and lose the childlike ability to enjoy the simplicity of life. Laughter and a light heart enliven our spirit and strengthen our physical bodies.

Following this corporate manifestation our church body returned to our typical joy drought. The laughter and lightness eluded us. It was during this time that I attended a men's retreat with a group of guys from my church. In one of the sessions, Bill Johnson spoke about encountering God. He stated that when you have an encounter with God, you then possess the key to the door of that experience whenever you need it. You don't have to wait for God to release the experience again; it is like a room in heaven to which you now have continual access. After Bill explained this, a light bulb went off in my head—I had the joy key!

When the session ended, I raced back to my room and jumped on my bunk bed, laughing. And even though it was still a bit dry, I knew I'd found the key to this heavenly door leading into joy. One of the men of our church attempted to nap and when he heard my laughter, he placed a pillow over his head. I leapt onto his bunk and laid my hands on him, all the while laughing. Little by little, laughter overcame him. Before long other men returned to our bunkroom and as we laid hands on them, the hilarity spread. By the end of our time together, a number of men walked through the door of this God encounter. As the encounter grew, people experienced visions, angelic visitations and prophetic utterances flowing out of them like a river. For the remainder of the retreat the "joy" encounter lingered and we leaked wherever we went. It did not end there, but followed us home and grew as we learned to steward this heavenly gift.

For some this may appear strange, "fleshy" or unbiblical. However, in the book of Acts when the Spirit was poured out on the day of Pentecost, the 120 present were accused of being drunk with wine at nine in the morning! Some, however, made fun of them and said, "*They have had too much wine. Then Peter stood up with the Eleven, raised his voice and addressed the crowd: "Fellow Jews and all of you who live in Jerusalem, let me explain this to you; listen carefully to what I say. These men are not drunk, as you suppose. It is only nine in the morning! No, this is what was spoken by the prophet Joel: "In the last days, God says, "I will pour out my Spirit on all people...* (Acts 2:13-17)

Sometimes what appears foolish in the eyes of others is simply a childlike response to God, much like my encounters at the men's retreat and Friday night service. God poured Himself out through the Holy Spirit and the overflow of that act resulted in joyful worship and declaring the goodness of God in what we labeled as "intoxication."

Joy is essential to walking in ongoing freedom. For those whose hearts and spirits are like dry wells, everything is serious—God is someone we tiptoe around. But for the person whose life overflows with abundant water, God is always good, kind, loving, faithful and even fun. True joy can only be sustained by the knowledge that God is not constantly angry with you. He is "...*slow to anger and abounding in love...*" (Nehemiah 9:17) Laughter, lightness and a correct view of God are key to sustaining joy. In the movie *Pollyanna* the transformed Reverend Ford said it like this, "Our visits with God on Sundays are going to be happier and more rejoicing, too."

In the next chapter we'll discover how thankfulness nurtures joy and how joy becomes a fortress of God's strength in our lives.

Chapter 13

The Little That Became Much

As I plunged deeper into the rabbit hole of hidden wonders, God revealed to me that in order to sustain joy I had to learn a lifestyle of thankfulness. While it was great to have an encounter of joy in His presence, I knew that if I didn't nurture a lifestyle of gratitude, I could not sustain this joy. The experience would quickly dissipate, causing me to return to my former life of exhaustion, discouragement and hopelessness. Gratitude was the foundation necessary to cultivate a vibrant life with God—the life that I greatly desired. Like Reverend Ford from the movie *Pollyanna*, after many years of negativity I had to learn how to view life from a distinct perspective. In one of Ford's sermons, he summed it up like this, "Let's go outside and enjoy this Sunday for a change and while you're out appreciating the sunlight, give a little thought to *Who* is sending it down to you."

At this time I still lived a meager existence merely tolerating the journey. Although God had blessed me with healthy relationships and a wonderful family, the process of expanding our financial base and creating a thriving church was something I did not embrace joyfully. Truthfully, I found it to be emotionally and spiritually draining and frequently felt depleted. My heart was not filled with the overflowing gratitude of God's love to lead me through my journey of life.

At one point in my life I was a pretty good cross-country runner, it was a sport at which I excelled. A primary reason for my success was my understanding of the importance of pacing. I had learned that starting too quickly made it difficult to sustain the pace all the way to the end. At some point along the way you burn out and the race is lost. Too bad I didn't carry that lesson into life, which I approached more like a sprint than a marathon! Eventually, as happens to so many people, I did lose strength and become weary and discouraged. As a result, it was much more gratifying to minister abroad than to deal with the pressing needs at home. So I was running around the globe, preaching, teaching, touching people for Jesus, while slowly, but surely, wearing myself out.

Many times I hit the proverbial runner's wall and did nothing but complain about my discomfort. I hated opposition and the resulting rejection I felt. It started to feel as though I were running through molasses! As you can imagine, no matter what situation arose in my life, positive or negative, I wasn't a happy camper.

Then God began to change my perspective on life. One day, while grumbling to one of my mentors about life's hardships, he began to laugh. Out of compliance, I responded with laughter as well. Initially I was just going through the motions, but ultimately I was overwhelmed by his merriment and fell on the ground bursting with laughter. It was then that I sensed the Lord's voice saying, "Keith, it's easy and fun." God released a new viewpoint, opening me up to His perspective of my circumstances. He helped me to remain thankful and to see how even the most arduous situations in life could be easy and light with Him by my side. Jesus said, *"For my yoke is easy, and my burden is light."* (Matthew 11:30)

I had committed to praying three to four hours a day for four things: Souls, healings, joy and financial breakthrough. Every day I contended with God for breakthrough in those areas. This kind of intense prayer kept me connected to and focused on what had not yet manifested. Although it is a viable form of prayer, that day God stopped me. It was as if He put His hand on my head and...Screech...I came to a halt. I had paced back and forth in the sanctuary praying loudly for breakthrough. He said, "Keith I want to teach you a different way of praying. I want you to learn the prayer of thanks. Begin to thank me for what I am doing in each of these four areas." So I began to thank Him, recounting the testimonies I could recall from those four areas. *Thank you, Lord, that last week we saw a lady saved and filled with the Holy Spirit, who spoke in tongues and became full of joy at the park. Thank you, Lord, that we had bills needing to be paid and unexpected checks arrived and the bills were paid. Thank-you, Lord, for the healing we saw recently of the hurt leg.*

As I began to thank Him for what He had already accomplished, I was overwhelmed, jumping up and down shouting, "God I am in full-fledged revival, I am in the abundance of your goodness!" I was inundated by His faithfulness and since that day I have ceased to pray for revival and instead spend the majority of my prayer life in thanksgiving for what He is already doing, which increases what He does all the more. Sometimes we become engulfed by problems and pray from a discouraged, hopeless and doubtful perspective, which renders our prayers ineffective. If we tend to see what He is *not* doing, then we will not possess the necessary strength to continue onward.

While teaching and leading worship at a training facility in the mountains, a lady who needed healing approached me. After visiting her primary care physician, she had been informed that there was no cure for her allergies. The physician advised her to leave the geographical area due to the severity of her reaction to the local environment. In spite of the fact that she had been prayed for many times by many people, she still was not well. I told her I would not pray for her. Instead, I suggested that she needed to thank the Lord and engage in worship. That evening I had just started to lead worship when I heard a shout from the audience—it was this same young lady. When I further investigated, she testified that her allergies had disappeared during the worship time even though no one had prayed for her. As she entered into God's presence with a thankful heart...He healed her. Thanksgiving is a powerful weapon!

During a very difficult financial season I learned a valuable lesson. I felt heavy and discouraged over our lack. To combat this, I spent time alone in my bedroom recounting testimonies of God's faithfulness in my life. I shouted out His faithfulness and goodness in my life. Let me be clear that God didn't need that...*I* did! I needed to strengthen myself in the Lord's faithfulness, so I thanked Him for coming through for me in a specific instance a couple of months earlier and then released a shout of praise. At that time, I honestly didn't feel much; no angelic presence or wonderful peace. A week later I received an unexpected, sizable check that covered our pressing bills and also provided a way for me to minister in a nation that had been on my heart. The Lord said, "That check resulted from the thanks you released a week ago."

Joel 1:16 says, *"Has not the food been cut off before our very eyes – joy and gladness from the house of our God?"* Have you ever been in a house where there was an empty refrigerator? I don't know about you, but that's not a house I'd want to spend a lot of time in. What is the benefit of a comfortable and spacious home without the joy and sustenance that comes from shared meals? In this passage, Joel points out that joy and gladness is the food that had been cut off from the house of God. We *are* that house. What was missing, then and now? Joy! There is no strength to transition from glory to glory without this joy. Thanks and gladness are foundational ingredients to experiencing a life of joy.

Jesus understood this key of thankfulness and used it many times. In Mark 6:41, He was facing five thousand hungry people in need of food with only five loaves of bread and a couple of fish to feed them. You know the story. *"Taking the five loaves and the two fish and looking up to heaven, he gave thanks and broke the loaves. Then he gave them to his disciples to set before the people. He also divided the two fish among them all."* Look at that simple act: His thankfulness for the *little* was the catalyst for multiplication and increase. Our act of thanksgiving for the *little* carries in it the answer for the *much*. John 6:23 says, *"Then some boats from Tiberias landed near the place where the people had eaten the bread after the Lord had given thanks."* Are you beginning to see how thanksgiving is a key to release abundance?

Many times we discount the little things God does because we have not witnessed a full-sized breakthrough. Meanwhile, God gazes at His beloved, patiently waiting to see if we are thankful for the little. As believers we desire to see cancer healed and the dead to be raised, but when God heals a headache do we wrap thanks around it? Hidden in the thanks for the healed headache is the ingredient for healed cancer. When I ask someone if they are feeling better after I've prayed and they respond with, "Not really, maybe a little," my reaction is not one of defeat or unbelief. Instead, I jump around with excitement and offer God thanks that we attained even a little measure of breakthrough. Because all we need is a little breakthrough. The beginning of a miracle is proof that the door to that heavenly answer has cracked open. When we become radically thankful for the first small signs of a miracle, a heavenly door swings wide open allowing the fullness of God total access to our lives.

How many miracles can we see through a thankful heart? Psalm 22:3 says, in the KJV, *"But thou are holy, o thou that inhabitest the praises of Israel."* The word *inhabitest* means to live, habitate, sit on. The word *praises* is the Hebrew word *tehilal*, in which the root word *halal* means "to boast, to be clamorously foolish, to rave." In other words, when you "go bonkers" over what God is doing—He comes and sits, lives on and inhabits those praises. Wherever God resides sickness, disease, poverty, lack, problems and disunity cannot exist. What an absolute privilege we have to always be on the lookout for the things great or small that God is doing.

It is like Elijah in 1 Kings 18:43-44, *Go and look toward the sea," he told his servant. And he went up and looked. "There is nothing there," he said. Seven times Elijah said, "Go back." The seventh time the servant reported, "A cloud as small as a man's hand is rising from the sea." So Elijah said, "Go and tell Ahab, 'Hitch up your chariot and go down before the rain stops you.* Elijah prayed with expectation that God would break in to the situation. All he needed was for his servant to see the smallest form of a cloud. As soon as his servant spotted a tiny cloud in the sky, Elijah knew he had his breakthrough. Being thankful for even the small things God is doing is the key to an abundant harvest.

Amos 9:11-13 says, *In that day I will restore David's fallen tent. I will repair its broken places, restore its ruins, and build it as it used to be, so that they may possess the remnant of Edom and all the nations that bear my name," declares the Lord, who will do these things. "The days are coming," declares the Lord, "when the reaper will be overtaken by the plowman and the planter by the one treading grapes. New wine will drip from the mountains and flow from all the hills.*

Amos speaks of a harvest of such abundance that the one who is planting overtakes the one reaping. Do you know that there is a place in the Spirit where we will harvest and reap simultaneously? That place is found at the restoration of the tent of David. David's tent was a place of thanksgiving, joy and praise for the goodness of God. David found a secret that we too can possess: Thanksgiving produces breakthrough, blessing, harvest and joy. When He is the delight of your life there will be abundance. How can you be discouraged when you dwell in David's tabernacle of praise?

Let me include one final story to illustrate the key of thanksgiving.

In Luke 24, two men were walking together after Jesus had died. They were discouraged and their faces downcast. In verses 15-17 we read, *As they talked and discussed these things with each other, Jesus himself came up and walked along with them; but they were kept from recognizing him. He asked them, "What are you discussing together as you walk along?" they stood still, their faces downcast.*

Notice that Jesus is with them and yet they did not recognize Him because they were downcast. Their vision was consumed with negativity; they could not see what He was doing, only what they had not yet seen—His resurrection. He walked with them for a while and then stopped for some food. Luke 24:30-31, *"When he was at the table with them, he took bread, gave thanks, broke it and began to give it to them. Then their eyes were opened and they recognized him, and he disappeared from their sight."* It was after thanksgiving was released that their eyes were opened.

How many situations are there in life where we miss the answer to our questions or the solutions to our problems simply because of discouragement or a negative focus? The solution to turning this around could be as simple as lifting up your eyes and giving thanks for the smallest of things you perceive Him doing. Who knows what possibilities lay right before you if you could only see them? I pray that a spirit of praise, thanks and radical joy would arise within you right now and that the garments of thanks and praise would cover you and heaviness would be removed. I pray that you would find the breakthrough that has been right at your fingertips the whole time, simply waiting to be recognized. Amen!

In this chapter we have considered how thanksgiving can change your viewpoint and infuse you with overflowing joy that results in breakthrough.

In the next chapter I want to dive into relationship issues and their connection to the lack of sustainable joy. We must develop a culture of healthy relationships that nurture joy and a vibrant faith.

Chapter 14

Relational Glue

The adhesive that holds together the revelation of His presence, power, and the *more* of God is relationship. I was taught growing up that as pastors it was unacceptable to be friends with the people in your congregation. And yet my parents routinely gave themselves to people they loved and pastored, often having people they befriended, including board members, turn on them. There were other times that my parents confided in fellow ministers only to be rejected by the ones to whom they had opened their hearts for help. Now, I do not want to paint a picture of complete bleakness in my upbringing because my parents did an amazing job with what they were given. They led many churches out of fractured states into a place of healing.

But the hurt I felt over seeing how they were treated caused me to resist being a pastor. I mean why would I want to put myself at that kind of risk? Truthfully, I had a beef with the church. It seemed to me that being in ministry meant always being surrounded by controlling, grumpy, cantankerous two-faced people. I was frustrated with congregations and pastors who simply did not get along.

The Lord told me that just having His presence and power in our midst fell short of His desire. Although these would most certainly attract people, they weren't the entirety of His fullness. If you do not foster a culture of relationship founded in honor, then people who come for His presence and power will bring division. People came to our church having left dry places and calling out for more. And these weren't just church hoppers; some had been leaders in their former churches. The common thread seemed to be that these people, though hungry and wounded, could no longer endure simple survival. Out of this group of people longing for a place to thrive came some mighty leaders.

I spent the first five years of pastoring learning how to love, how to maintain honor in disagreement and how to contend with my enemies. Some of my dearest friends were the very ones who left the church causing much division. Ironically, I wrestled with the same wounds as my parents. Being accustomed to a strong, one-man leadership style, I was not stellar at navigating relationships. This fact was readily evident in my relationship with my wife, where I had learned at a young age that a wife's job was to be a good support for her husband, the "Minister." Every relationship role revolved around congregants learning to honor the one man and his vision. This is a great deal of power and control to give one person and it is certainly not the Lord's model for a thriving church. This model of leadership creates the very atmosphere where undermining—gossip, backbiting, criticism, suspicion, lack of trust toward leadership and unteachability—thrives. I had experienced the sting of these poisonous arrows aimed at my family while growing up.

I recall one particular meeting where my parents were subjected to what is commonly called a "vote of confidence." They had pastored the church for several years and according to the church bylaws, every year a vote was taken to determine if the congregation wanted them to continue in pastoral leadership. Because my brothers and I were young adult voting members, we were allowed at the meeting...but my parents were not. There was an open microphone up in the front for corporate discussion before the final vote was cast. One woman, who played an active role in undermining my parent's leadership stood, took the microphone and spoke against my parents, publicly criticizing their ministry. At one point my twin brother, Kevin, who simply could not cope with her accusations, jumped to his feet and began publicly refuting her. She disagreed and he, once again refuted her. This went back and forth for several minutes graphically demonstrating the painful truth that while people seemed quite willing to negatively disagree publically, there wasn't the same level of willingness to meet together privately and work out differences. I loathed membership meetings for this very reason.

The woman in question ended up leaving the church and taking a handful of people with her. But my parents, being the gracious servants that they were, continued to love her and those who had chosen to leave with her. Some of those folks eventually returned, only to leave in bitterness again a few years later. I now believe that the Lord allowed these painful experiences so that when I finally did pastor my own church I would be strategic in how I approached building DNA; that I'd be careful to provide a wineskin free from such dysfunctions.

During this period of growth, Kris Vallotton told me that I was great at dealing with my enemies, but terrible at dealing with my friends. He told me that I ended up making my friends my enemies in order to deal with them. Ouch! I didn't know how to foster true relationships, nor did I realize at the time that a huge part of the dysfunction in the church was the control granted to the one man at the top. Control breeds undermining. These spirits work hand in hand. Where there is division in the body against leadership, there is control. When people do not feel empowered or that their needs are being met, they will find a way to be heard. The sad part is that they will most likely hurt other individuals in the process. The Lord in His wisdom has set up a relational pattern designed for cohesive flow between a leadership team and the congregation.

In order to preserve a hierarchal leadership style, there must be words like "submission" in play. Therefore, in order to remove my controlling leadership style, the Lord addressed my long-term issue of submission. While submission is a Biblical term, it is quite often wrongly used to keep people under control and has been severely abused by many in positions of authority. Over time it has become the congregation's job to submit to the vision of leadership much in the same way that I saw my wife's job being to submit to my decisions. It might sound biblical, but a pure heart is suspect here.

I played the submission card because I feared people. Having watched people hurt my parents; I had subconsciously vowed that I would never allow that kind of hurt to touch my heart! And when I began pastoring, I kept a sharp eye on anyone who questioned my decisions or did not fully embrace my vision. I developed subtle ways of removing opposition from the camp, cleaning up the membership roster, so as to only have "true supporters" on our list. I did not realize how many people I hurt in the process of attempting to protect myself from pain.

After the Lord revealed to me the damage I had produced, I spent considerable amount of time repenting for my hurtful actions. I am thankful the Lord graciously allowed me to pastor in a place where, overall, people loved me. The compassionate people, with whom the Lord encircled me, would fight to the death with me for the Kingdom we discovered was available to us. What God built during those years in Willits was not something I did alone, but something we built together by His grace. The Lord was more interested in creating new DNA in my spirit and the spirits of others around me than He was in large numbers. He knew that the foundations must be secure before the building could handle great numbers. I am thankful for what I learned in those years of leadership. I take these lessons with me all around the world and they have impacted many lives. I do not despise the day of these small beginnings; rather, I am grateful for the Lord's careful choice of where I developed relational values.

During this season I had to learn that I was not called to keep people on my arm, tethered like hawks. I had to release them to fly. One of the first prophetic words given to me featured a vision of my wife perched on my arm like a hawk. The lady prophesying remarked that I would release Heather, but she eventually had to return to my arm because I controlled her. God did not want such behavior on my part, nor did He design the concept of submission to be used in this way.

As I mentioned in chapter one, the first time I saw Heather she was dancing before the Lord during a worship service at Bible College. No one else dared to dance in that thousand seat auditorium...except

Heather. Spiritually speaking, she was well ahead of me in her passion for the Lord. She had already attended many revival meetings with Rodney Howard Browne and other revivalists of that time. As you are aware, I stood completely against what I thought was spiritual "hype" of any kind. When I informed Heather that she was arrogantly showing off in front of many people, I shut down dance as a form of her worship expression for many years. In fact, her friends questioned why she would even desire to marry me, but she saw something in me under all the entrenched religion and control.

Someone worth marrying.

I am exceedingly thankful for my marvelous wife, who now dances so beautifully in worship. It still took several years for Heather to truly and freely dance again, a fact for which I have repented repeatedly. But I learned a truth that you would do well to remember: Controlling leadership exacts a heavy toll from those over whom it exerts power.

The leadership model acquired from my church circles had one man at the top, and *that* man was to be feared; the one to whom you listened; the one who held all the cards. Many that I admired walk in this leadership style resulting in their leadership being undermined in the churches where they served. I knew there must be another way. However, it is hard to let go of control when it is all you have ever known. For me, releasing the control card meant embracing others emotionally and trusting that I would not get hurt beyond repair.

Many people had exited our church and there were only a handful of us left when we began the rebuilding process. But we were hungry and lived for the presence and power of God. One of our first new families was a lovely couple with several children who had been quality leaders in another church—a church where they had remained committed for years. Yet, something inside of them felt *there must be more*. We immediately formed a connection but, unfortunately, it wasn't long before we, along with others in our church, became suspicious of them. They exhibited similar behaviors and characteristics of the people who had left our church...people who had deeply hurt us. Would they do the same? This family had to blaze a trail into our church with courage, cutting through the walls of fear we had erected. Eventually they broke through into our hearts.

The Lord taught me how to identify areas in my past that required healing, illuminating my hesitancy to trust in areas where I had been previously hurt. Having watched my parents repeatedly wronged by hurtful relationships and having experienced pain myself at the hand of close friends and church members, it was now time to come full circle. I needed to have successful, enduring relationships so that I could develop the capacity to lead our church into a relationally healthy place. We saw an influx of new members who loved the presence, worship and power that flowed through our meetings, but they would only stay if we created a way to love, honor and value one another without fear or control.

Pastor and author Danny Silk played a significant role in developing the relational culture of our church. I knew that he had honed in on my distorted view of submission when he said, "Keith, if you ever have to use the submission card on your wife or church, you are not truly the one in charge. A true leader does not lead with threats or scripture verses held over people's heads. A true leader serves. Your job is to serve your wife, find out how to make her succeed and find out how to help your leadership staff and church succeed."

At this time, I permitted my wife to dream and encouraged her to follow these dreams...to a point. As soon as I became uncomfortable with her dreams I shut her down with the submission card. I would say something like, "Dear, you can't do this anymore. I am not enjoying myself and your endeavor is making me uncomfortable," and her dream would be completely sabotaged.

Heather dearly loves people and is a go-getter with uncanny leadership skills. She loves working with a team and easily empowers others by ascertaining and utilizing their strengths. She's a party animal! Socialization actually refreshes and refuels her and as a result, people gravitate to her. I, on the other hand, like to have a good deal of private time. Don't get me wrong, I like being with my family, but after ministering to others I will eventually need to retreat to my cave to recuperate for the next ministry stint.

I must admit that my main issue with Heather running off and pursuing her dreams had to do with the loneliness I felt. While she was buzzing around chasing the desires of her heart, I was stuck at home. That couldn't be right! So, eventually I would become angry at her absence from home and pull the plug on her dreams. Remember, I was walking in the only leadership style I knew: I am the man, the man is the boss and my word is final. And though it pains me to say it, like a flower plucked from the soil, she wilted under my control. Of course, I felt terrible, but the damage was already done.

Learning to let go and allow Heather to follow her dreams was challenging, but I eventually saw the light. I learned to be truthful about my feelings, willing to confess my concerns about what each new adventure would bring us. Most importantly, I learned that if it was a dream of Heather's heart, I needed to get behind it one hundred percent. Not simply because she wanted to do it, but because I loved her and desired that she fulfill her dreams. As Heather's dreams were fulfilled, our marriage was enhanced and we became more effective as a ministry couple.

Being a visionary with a strong prophetic voice made letting go in the church difficult as well. One afternoon I entered one of our leadership meetings where I had empowered our leaders to share from their hearts. I began to share the vision I wanted to target in a certain area—a vision I had heard from the Lord. The problem was that I presented it more as a "done deal" than a topic for discussion and development. One leader confronted me on the spot about the vision, saying, "Keith, you haven't even given us time to discuss this or to think it through properly." That was tough for me to receive, but I eventually began to value and truly hear my leaders, encouraging them to express their ideas, understanding that leaders buy into things they create.

The Lord spoke to me once and said, "Keith, it is not your job to come up with the vision for your church. It is your job to speak into your congregation and out of them will flow the vision." *So let me get this straight, God...my job is to pull the dreams from inside our people and then help fulfill those dreams?* That was a radically new idea to me! Nevertheless, I immediately began working to create a Kingdom culture with core values that drove everything we did. Along with our team of leaders, I worked to define and protect those values. Every meeting we held, no matter how big or small—board meetings, leadership meetings, public meetings, home groups, outreaches—had to have three things in mind: We wanted the presence of God in everything we touched; we wanted to see His power in every meeting; and everything had to be done within the context of honorable relationships.

Learning to facilitate the vision of the church leaders—finding out where they fit, their passions, how they excelled or faltered—was key to building a successful team. Let me just tell you that it was no minor task. As time progressed, we began to find success in small ways. We not only became friends with the people in our church, but we found ways to help realize some of their potential.

After we'd been there about seven years, new associates came to help us develop the church. They too had experienced hurtful church situations, but found true relationship and nurture for their dreams in our culture. We spent a great deal of time trying to move them into areas of passion versus areas of duties. We told them we did not want them serving because there was a job to be done, but that we wanted them working in areas where they shined. They found that place. In fact, they developed areas in the church where Heather and I lacked the talent and vision to do so. This was definitely a huge win in the area of becoming an empowering leader versus a controlling leader.

People on the outside who had been skeptical of this new move of God began to take note of our healthy leadership style. An individual remarked, "One thing we do see is the fruit of love that Keith and his church have for each other." We learned how to move out of dysfunctional relationships into relationships of love that cultivated empowerment, encouraging people to pursue their God-given purpose.

One key to breaking down the dividing walls between the people and leadership was revealed when the Lord gave me deeper revelation and insight into scripture. I had viewed God as a stern, distant father and that mindset formed my style of leadership. However, as my view of God transformed so did my leadership style. I remember the Lord giving me Ephesians 4:3-6, *Make every effort to keep the unity of the Spirit through the bond of peace. There is one body and one Spirit — just as you were called to one hope when you were called- one Lord, one faith, one baptism; one God and Father of all, who is over all and through all and in all.*

God said, "Keith, you stand *alongside* the people in your church. You are not above them. You are *one* with them. You all start in a place of unity in Christ. It is not something you strive for; it is something you obtain when you come into Christ. There is no separation. Yes, you are the leader and if you empower them to the point where you have no power that is no good either."

Another passage of scripture that helped to change the way I viewed my relationship with others was Galatians 3:27-28, *For all of you who were baptized into Christ have clothed yourselves with Christ. There is neither Jew nor Greek, slave nor free, male nor female, for you are all one in Christ Jesus.* This passage pertains to how we relate to one another. Because we are in Christ and Christ is in us, we no longer separate ourselves from one another through any division: No racial division, class division, job division, gender division, or even age division. We are all one in Christ and together we stand before the Lord. Leaders do not stand at a higher place with the Lord than everyone else. We are all ministers, friends and priests of God who need to learn to stand as friends together in life; to fight against seeing each other according to the way the world sees each other.

The world's system teaches us from a young age to size people up according to position, clothing, money or lack thereof, as well as many other factors. For me, the title *leader* and *pastor* separated me from the people in my church. It was either them...or me. I didn't realize that

God wanted there to be an "us." God modeled this perfect unity in Jesus' prayer in John 17:22, *"I have given them the glory that you gave me, that they may be one as we are one."* The Godhead is made up of three distinct parts that are perfectly one. There are unique job descriptions that each carry, but in the end it is a perfect union. We are called to emulate this picture of the Godhead. We are already one and have to fight to keep the unity given to us through Christ.

I remember people hosting unity meetings in our city, meetings that were led by some of the people who had left our church—people who had released many critical words about us everywhere they went. Many believers attended these meetings and we participated as well. Yet, many considered us untrustworthy and spiritually questionable. I went because I would not let anything keep us hidden, including scornful words. In the end, there was no true unity at these meetings, only suspicion toward us and toward one another. True unity never begins at a meeting, but begins in Christ and then continues in relationships of honor. Then, and only then can meetings take place that are truly unified. The goal is not big meetings; the goal is hearts that love and care for one another without condition or even the exact same beliefs. The fundamental foundations of the Gospel remain critical, but peripheral preferences don't have to be agreed on to have true unity.

Another part of successful unity lies in the leader's grasp of true authority. Scripture tells us in 2 Corinthians 13:10, *This is why I write these things when I am absent, that when I come I may not have to be harsh in my use of authority – the authority the Lord gave me for building you up, not for tearing you down.* Godly authority is not to be used to control people, but to serve one another in love. Jesus says in Matthew 20:25-26, *"You know that the rulers of the Gentiles lord it over them, and their high officials exercise authority over them. Not so with you. Instead, whoever wants to become great among you must be your servant.*

True authority is seen in someone who lives to lift another up, someone who lives to help another shine. Jesus is the ultimate example of this. Ephesians 5:25 says, *"Husbands, love your wives, just as Christ loved the church and gave himself up for her..."* Christ did not lord it over those to whom He was called. Instead, He served the church in such a way that He gave His life up for her. When someone models Christ's example of leadership, it is not hard for others to submit. I have heard it said by many at Bethel church in Redding, California that submission means to come under the *mission* of those you serve. You cannot truly go forward into your destiny, until you truly submit...and you are not truly submitting until you understand the *mission* of the leadership you serve and the core values that they fight for. Once you whole-heartedly submit to those values — once you understand them, believe in them and fight for them — *then* you can be commissioned into your purpose.

We had hungry folks flocking to us who loved the mission of our church. They loved our core values and the presence and power of God. However, some were initially hesitant to submit and be willing to entrust themselves to someone who could speak into their lives and invest the time required for spiritual development. To truly submit means that you trust those whom God has placed over you; you don't just adhere to their values in word, but also in heart. Once you have the heart of that leader then true submission begins that will commission you to your God designed assignment.

In order for you to be receiving your church's blessing and be sent out into your destiny you first have to trust in and be connected with those whom God has given as your overseers. Leaders who use their leadership position to serve the body in love are the ones worthy of building the Kingdom.

In the next chapter I will discuss the kind of relational skills that must be in place to build an army of love-filled, Kingdom-advancing Christians. Without the right foundations in relationships the Church cannot withstand opposition, but with a unified body of people submitting one to another as unto the Lord, she will be unstoppable.

Chapter 15

The Connection Doctor

Having a working understanding of the tools necessary for nurturing healthy connections is vital to long-term Kingdom success. Each one of us desires to be in relationships where we are cared for and where we can care for others. In this chapter I want to address some of the relationship keys I learned along the way.

As I shared in the previous chapter, building healthy relationships was not an easy task within the context of being a pastor's kid and it certainly didn't change when I began to pastor. Navigating friendships with the people in my congregation required a gear, or a revelation, if you will, that I simply did not have. But thank God I had mentors who cared enough to stick by me until I began to not only achieve healthy connections but had also acquired the skills needed to keep those connections alive.

The issue of building significant relationships was one that took several years to unravel, i.e. I didn't know how to turn on the connection spout and how to turn it off; when to talk, with whom to talk and how much to say. I made many mistakes in my attempts to usher people into my inner circle and then entrust them with details of my heart — details they often had no grace to handle. I found that many attempted to fix me, which proved hurtful. Or worse yet, they divulged to other church members what I had shared with them in private.

I was not in search of relationships that would fix my problems; I had great mentors to help me navigate those waters. Instead, I searched for friends who would understand and accept me. This was one of the most challenging lessons as a young pastor desiring healthy connection. Who will appreciate my gifting? Who will handle my style of leadership? Who will accept my outward processing? What parts of me can I give away to others? I had learned a key from King David early on: He was vulnerable before the Lord *and* others. I understood that the Lord delights in our vulnerability, however, I did not realize that most of what I processed internally was too much for others to handle in the context of friendship. I spent many years going into meetings with various leadership teams and baring my heart only to have them perform "open heart surgery" without anesthesia! I did not grasp that I had yet to find a safe environment with the right people to whom I could unveil my inner thoughts and feelings.

People process things one of two ways: Internally or outwardly. With me, it's all outward. Outward processors are those who require dialogue to sort out what is churning in their thoughts and emotions. And because I longed for a place of true openness through dialogue, every week I jumped into the deep end of the swimming pool, barely clothed, while others stood at the edge *fully* clothed. In other words, I poured out my heart...and everyone observed without reciprocating.

I did experience wonderful freedom at a six-week worship camp during this season of searching for healthy connection. Over the course of those six weeks, I found freedom to speak my heart and was accepted in doing so. I tried to build this same culture at my home church and, sadly, it did not fly because I didn't realize the extent to which I needed to be intentional with what I was creating in our core culture. One of the keys in creating this culture was the need to verbally define the intent of specific conversations between leaders and between friends. Was this a conversation about something that needed to be fixed; a conversation where someone simply needed to be heard; or was it a conversation that needed to be saturated with prayer? In my case, I routinely verbalized the issues of my life as a means of working through my thoughts. Quite often, at the end of a conversation I would discover the answer that had previously eluded me. As an outward processor, I just needed a sounding board. I suspect that this is why as a nation we spend so much money on therapists. Many people do not have friends and mentors who will simply listen to them and I'm sure you would agree that being heard is one of the most deeply felt needs in our society.

I began to identify individuals who had the grace to lend an ear as I poured out the intimate details of my life. This resulted in every part of my life being heard...but not by one person. I had friends and mentors with whom I could share my struggles as a man—purity issues, thoughts on the challenge of pastoring, marriage, finances and child rearing—but I couldn't share the struggles with my congregation with just anyone. I needed a safe place...individuals who possessed wisdom and the ability to not take sides or cast judgment against the people who were frustrating me. My mentors and others not associated with our church body initially filled this role. But eventually I found an incredible individual within the church that could handle all the good, the bad and the ugly of Keith Ferrante. Everyone needs to have someone who can see you on your worst day and still love and respect you; someone who will allow you to release all the junk and all the pain from your system so that God can begin the healing process. If there is no place for release, things tend to fester and over time become hazardous to *your* health and infectious to others.

I once led a men's group that provided me with a tremendous opportunity to try duplicating this culture of connection. We were studying the book, *Wild at Heart,* by John Eldredge and I had worked very hard to create a safe environment for the men to externally process the struggles that every man endures, but few ever voice. I would tell them every week, "Guys, when someone shares, we are not going to fix them, pray for them, or feel sorry for them. We are simply here to listen and support them." Do you know how hard that is for men? Most guys are fixers. We love to discover or create solutions to problems, so to see something broken and not try to fix it, goes against everything we are. However, within a culture of connection you have to know when to offer a solution, when to simply listen and when to pray. Sometimes you just need to find the courage to tell someone in advance what kind of a conversation you most need to have.

When Heather and I learned this lesson it brought tremendous tranquility to our communication. Early in our marriage we constantly offered suggestions to each other that we thought helpful. Truthfully though, when Heather attempted to fix my problems, or vice versa, it produced nothing but conflict. I would become defensive, lashing out at her because it seemed to me that she wasn't really backing me up... she wasn't *for* me. Nothing could have been further from the truth! In hindsight, I should've had the courage to say to Heather, "Even though I may not have done well in my sermon today, I don't really want to be *fixed*, I just need encouragement." Over time as she began to honor my need for affirmation, I, in turn, started trusting her to speak into areas where I really needed help.

Proverbs 11:12 says, "*A man who lacks judgment derides his neighbor, but a man of understanding holds his tongue.*" There is a time for everything; a time to speak wisdom and a time to hold our tongue. Not understanding what "time" it is can be damaging to relationships. You may have great wisdom, but unless you are *invited* to speak into the hearts of others, you will trample boundaries causing people to build walls to keep you out instead of constructing bridges to allow you access. In order for us to find healthy relationships, we must be willing to maintain our boundaries and respect the boundaries of others.

Boundaries are another crucial element in building a culture of connection. When we are brought up in a controlling environment where boundaries have been dictated by an authority figure, we have a tough time creating healthy boundaries for ourselves. A child who is neither heard nor respected tends to develop emotional barriers to help cope with boundaries that are being trampled. Even as adults, if we are not heard and respected the tendency will be to check out mentally and emotionally.

My parents did a great job of raising us and the fact that I serve God today is a testimony to their parenting skills. And yet my brother continually tested the waters of individuality by attempting to voice his own opinions, an action that was met with strong opposition from our father, who was always the boss. It has been my observation that whenever a child's paradigm includes a dominant parental figure, it will either produce a tendency to undermine authority, or an emotional woundedness. Having seen my brother encounter "the wrath of dad," I learned to internalize my feelings becoming a people pleaser, a skill I carried into pastoring. And can you guess how that affected my relationships? Now *I* held the authority card. *I* was the boss. Learning to verbalize my boundaries instead of internalizing them and blowing out relationships with harsh confrontations was a painful lesson.

Kris Vallotton was right: I *was* great at handling my enemies and terrible at handling my friends. That reality played out something like this: I would not address my frustrations in a particular relationship, which ultimately propelled me to a breaking point. I would build an increasingly large case in my mind against them until I finally detached myself emotionally. Then I would call the individual into the office and reel off everything they had done wrong. As you can probably imagine, by that point, it was very difficult to heal the relationship.

I remember Danny Silk coming to our church to speak about relationships during a season when I was struggling with a particular individual. My issue had to do with the flattering way he spoke to me and his insistence in hugging me in a manner I deemed inappropriate. There was nothing perverse about it, it just made me uncomfortable. Danny said, "Keith, you need to be truthful about what you need. Request that he not flatter you with his words and not hug you until you feel safe." I wrestled with gaining the courage to share this. I was the pastor, and aren't pastors supposed to be loving and caring to everyone in their congregation? Yes, and no. I learned that, like everybody else, I was a human being with viable thoughts, feelings and boundaries. When I encountered things that hurt me or made me feel uncomfortable, I needed to intentionally speak up.

Like clockwork, the individual approached me to conduct our usual uncomfortable conversation. But before he could get near me I physically withdrew. Well, actually, I jerked away. You see, I had held off for so long in sharing my boundaries that my response was rather extreme. I stopped, turned and said, "I know this may not sit well with you but I do not feel encouraged and loved when you hug and talk to me the way you do. I know this is probably just me, but I need you not to give me any compliments or hug me until I feel safe." Danny informed me ahead of time that it was highly likely that this individual would become upset, a typical result when boundaries are introduced to existing relationships. It takes bravery to walk out of unhealthy relational dynamics. Danny was spot on. The individual became angry and argued that this was not how he treated me. His wife stood next to him, sheepishly agreeing with me. She feared his wrath as well. I stood firm in my boundary declaring, "I am sure your heart is right in this matter, but the boundary I have drawn is what I need in order to feel safe in this relationship."

Establishing boundaries was only the first step in changing the confrontational history I had with this individual. He wanted to get to know me better, but I told him if he wanted to have a closer friendship he had to begin by honoring my boundaries. This wasn't easy for either one of us. It seemed like every week for a solid year I had to redraw the boundary. Every meeting we attended together, he continued with the same old behavior and each time I had to remind him of what we discussed regarding my boundary. He argued, but I persisted. I had a constant nagging lie that had been with me many years. *You do not love enough, Keith. You need to love more.* I had to persistently deny this lie and declare that I was loved and could love in return with good boundaries. Over time, the constant resistance wore me down to the point that one particular Sunday God had to send an angel to reaffirm to me that the boundaries I had established were from the Lord. Boundaries are designed to keep the good in and the bad out. I was accustomed to allowing life to just happen to me, which is exactly how I treated others as well. Not only did I have to value myself enough to draw my own boundaries...I had to learn to respect the boundaries of others.

Around this same time, there was a woman in our church who walked in subtle rebellion against the ways of the Lord—living in immoral relationships while at the same time trying to appear morally pure. Even though we walked her through counsel, attempted to cast out demons and engaged in many other attempts to see her freed, she refused to change. She constantly alleged that she was free; that she was trying her best and that she was walking clean. Three years of her continually disrupting the spiritual climate of our church produced an obvious undermining of our authority. At the same time, I still had the lie circulating through my head that I just needed to love her more.

I spoke with one of my mentors who said, "Keith, you are one of the most loving pastors I know. You need to get this lady out of your church." With fear and trembling, Heather and I had a conversation with her during which we told her she needed to leave the church until she was truly ready to change. Weeping, she begged us to let her stay and told us that she was changing. I responded "No, I don't think so; you need to leave this church." She left with loud shouts and anger mixed with self-pity and attempted manipulation. When she was completely off the property it was like the sky became bluer, things felt lighter...something had shifted in the atmosphere. I did not realize what a spiritual weight this woman's resistance had become for me. But when I finally stepped into my God-given authority the spiritual climate changed.

Jesus modeled the importance of boundaries with one of His disciples. Following the praise Jesus gave Peter in Matthew 16:16-18, for recognizing that He was the Son of God, Peter over-stepped a boundary when he attempted to block Jesus from pursuing His purpose on earth. Matthew 16:21-23, *From that time on Jesus began to explain to his disciples that he must go to Jerusalem and suffer many things at the hands of the elders, chief priests and teachers of the law, and that he must be killed and on the third day be raised to life. Peter took him aside and began to rebuke him. "Never, Lord!" he said. "This shall never happen to you!" Jesus turned and said to Peter, "Get behind me, Satan! You are a stumbling block to me; you do not have in mind the things of God, but the things of men.* Jesus believed in Peter, but had no problem correcting him when needed. If we desire a culture of connection we must develop the ability to have loving confrontations.

Where there is a supernatural, presence-driven culture people feel the freedom of heaven, which releases them to pray for others, prophesy and pursue dreams. If a presence-driven culture is not balanced by a relational culture, where confrontation is a necessary core value, then messes occur that no one cleans up. We end up hurting the very people who come for the presence and power because we do not know how to bring them into health. People learn healthy boundaries by having healthy boundaries modeled to them. People learn honor by those who demonstrate honor to them. When we've set boundaries with people and they do not respect them, steps must be taken to limit their influence in the realm of authority God has entrusted to us.

Another relational key and crucial element in building a culture of connection is the teachable heart. If someone is teachable it doesn't matter how much junk they have, there is always hope. I asked Bethel's worship leader, Brian Johnson, once what he looked for in a musician to be a part of the worship team. He told me that the main thing is teachability, because a teachable person is a moldable person.

I recall that during the early days of developing worship teams myself; I had some very talented young men and women around me. While I loved and appreciated their musical skills, some of them just were not teachable. They displayed the attitude that said they knew all there was to know about music and didn't really care to hear about ways to improve. After bumping heads with them for some time, I recognized that unless they were teachable they were not good candidates for leadership roles. I could still love them, but they would not be given a position of authority in the church until they understood this principle.

As we developed our church's leadership team this relational key grew more important. As an effective leader you constantly search for other leaders to fit the diverse positions needed to serve the church body. For the first few years I placed people into positions from which I would later have to remove them because they made too many messes and would not learn how to clean them up. Their placement had been based on their gifting instead of the visible fruit in their lives.

I appointed one particular individual as a leader for a period of several years — someone who was incredibly gifted in his area of ministry. As our relationship developed, he consistently asked for greater input from me. It did not matter how much affirmation I lavished on him or how many resources I offered...it was never enough. It finally climaxed when I fell under extreme exhaustion, distraught over my inability to sufficiently nurture his ministry. I pleaded with the Lord for more love. Surely, more love was the answer.

I invited leaders to speak into my life regarding this situation. Their opinion echoed the Lord's words to me. "Keith, the answer is not love. The answer is teachability." Then he took me to Proverbs 9:7-8, *Whoever corrects a mocker invites insult; whoever rebukes a wicked man incurs abuse. Do not rebuke a mocker or he will hate you; rebuke a wise man and he will love you.*

The word "mocker," or fool, means to be unteachable. The Lord revealed that when you try to teach someone who is unteachable, you set yourself up for hurt and failure. An unteachable person will constantly lash out, causing you to feel like *you* are the problem. The Lord went on to say, "Keith, the unteachability comes from a lack of trust in their life. An unteachable person is someone you can certainly continue to love but not someone you can work with in high levels of ministry." That revelation was definitely unexpected, as I had always assumed that the need was just for me to show more love.

Nevertheless, like refreshing water to a weary traveler, I eagerly received God's word. Praise the Lord the issue of growth in this case didn't come in the way I expected. I did *not* need to love more. I needed discernment to identify those capable of working with me and could handle my leadership style; those with enough trust in their heart to let me take them places they may not see for themselves. This revelation freed me to relieve the individual in question of his duties. He remained in the church and I continued to find ways to build into his life with trust and love. I knew this person was useful in the Kingdom; I had just misunderstood the timing and extent of their readiness.

Most of the people I worked with were ones who had trust issues. They had been hurt at some point by friends, fathers, spiritual mentors, leaders or churches...just as I had. There was the occasional bumping of heads as I learned which individuals were ready for leadership and which ones simply were not. As the old saying goes, "You can lead a horse to water but you can't make it drink." Some people are not ready to take steps into healthy connections and trusting relationships. I understand this well because I have been one of those people. Each new level of trust requires us to let go of control in our lives and be convinced that God is good. You have to know that God has plans to prosper you and not to harm you. Jeremiah 29:11 says, *"For I know the plans I have for you," declares the Lord, "plans to prosper you and not to harm you, plans to give you hope and a future."*

God wants you to trust His goodness to provide wonderful, trustworthy relationships with friends, leaders, sons and daughters. Even though some of you may have more work ahead of you than others, each of you has the capacity to create healthy relationships and a culture of connection. Allow the Lord to speak into areas where you have walled up your heart against others. If you are going to have good relationships you must be willing to let Him deal with your fears, hurts and disappointments. Pain isn't inevitable, but even if it does come, it is well worth the risk—even friends wound each other. Proverbs 27:6 says, *"Wounds from a friend can be trusted, but an enemy multiplies kisses."*

The Lord did not promise a pain free existence, but He *did* promise a fulfilling existence. You will not truly be fulfilled without healthy relationships consisting of lifelong friends, family and spiritual fathers and mothers. It is not easy developing those relationships. Several years ago when I moved from pastoring in Willits to Vacaville, California, I had to start over. The Mission is bigger and I am not the primary leader. The dynamics of our lives changed and we had the opportunity to use these relational tools repeatedly as we began to develop new connections. We learned that we could not wait for others to initiate relationships, but we had to be intentional about developing healthy connections. Though it takes time to find those you can fully trust and embrace in friendship, the benefits are immeasurable.

Once again, joyful, trustworthy and caring friends surround us. We have also found leaders in this body who care about us and from whom we receive correction, direction and encouragement. What a joy it is to be in a body where these elements are present. There is potential for great relationships everywhere when you utilize these tools to develop a culture of connection. I pray that you will move beyond your fears into a place of healthy life and abundance.

In the final chapter, I would like to focus on enjoying life. We discussed a bit about healthy relationships and now I want to study the attributes of a person who is a healthy person in mind, body and spirit. A healthy person is a prosperous person and prosperity is one of God's goals for us.

Chapter 16

Healthy Heart or Sick Soul

In the previous chapter we talked about understanding some of the vital relational keys necessary to sustain a strong life. In this chapter I would like to help you step into health in *every* area of your life, because a healthy life is one that will be a victorious life in the long run.

I suppose it'd be accurate to say that I approach life situations with everything I have, whether it is witnessing, praying, worshiping, playing instruments or playing sports; whatever I do, I do it passionately. Passion is a great attribute, but passion exhibited in limited areas of life can create a lack of health in other areas. We are challenged in scripture to keep it simple. David says in Psalm 27:4, *One thing I ask of the Lord, this is what I seek: that I may dwell in the house of the Lord all the days of my life, to gaze upon the beauty of the Lord and to seek him in his temple.*

I love the Lord with all my heart. Receiving and giving Him love is my primary assignment. God certainly loves those whose hearts are fully devoted to Him. In fact, He searches for them. However, the extreme tendencies of my personality led me to become a bit unbalanced.

I remember a discussion Heather and I had about my workload as we were driving back from a meeting in Redding. We wrote down every area in which I had invested time. Then next to each area we listed how many hours I spent on each one of those categories. We wrote down prayer time, sermon preparation, church meetings, worship time and connection with other pastors or leaders. The total amount of time I was investing in those areas amounted to approximately eighty hours per week (a standard nine to five job would be in the forty hour range, give or take a few hours). Oddly enough, I had an intense feeling of satisfaction when I learned how much I was working. This was largely due to the fact that my significance at the time was directly tied to the amount of time I was investing.

I didn't spend a lot of time counseling or seeing people during the average week. Most of my day, often up to eight hours, was invested in just spending time with Jesus—playing the piano, reading the Word, reading a thought provoking book, or just soaking in His presence. This was not something that was difficult or painful for me to do for it flowed from a place of joy.

One day I sensed the Lord saying, "Keith, I want you to have a regular forty hour workweek like many people who do not serve in vocational ministry have. I want those forty hours to include all your devotional time with me as well." *What am I going to do with my life, Papa? I will have so much free time.* He said, "I want you to spend time enjoying your son and daughter, your wife and your friends."

The first week of this change was a little overwhelming because I simply did not know what to do with all the additional hours in my day. I actually found myself feeling insignificant because I was not constantly in the prayer room. Heather encouraged me, "Keith, you have to see ministry as much bigger than your time spent in the worship room. You have to see ministry as spending time with your family, having fun and enjoying friends." Her statement was extremely challenging. Even though I had witnessed the tragedies of ministers who gave their all for the church and lost their families as a result, I was headed down that same path. As I began to spend quality time with my children, I gained a greater depth of what it meant to be a son; what it meant to relax and allow Dad to be the strong one; what it meant to enjoy life and allow Him to bless me. I found that I struggled with accepting God's blessing without feeling obligated to give back.

During this time the Lord also said, "Keith, I want you to be generous." His instruction confused me because I felt like an extremely generous person. He said, "I want you to be generous to *yourself*, Keith."

You see, I constantly gave away everything I received. If someone gave me money, I would sow it into someone else. In fact, it was around this time that I complained to the Lord about not having sufficient money to buy Christmas gifts for my children. He said, "Last week I provided you with an extra hundred dollars and you gave it away within a few minutes of receiving it." I began to realize that I was not giving out of true generosity, but out of my lack of understanding God's desire to bless me. I had to first learn how to receive in order to truly give. When I realized that every dollar the Lord gave me I had given away, I repented.

A few days later I received a check in the mail for five hundred dollars—a small inheritance from a dear friend who had recently passed away. When I was in college she had taken the time to mentor and disciple me, sharing the wisdom she'd gained through over fifty years in the ministry. Having viewed me as a spiritual son, the "widow's mite" inheritance was her way of passing on her spiritual mantle to me. I was truly overwhelmed by God's generosity and knew exactly how to spend the money. I bought Christmas gifts, gave some money to Heather to buy Christmas gifts and was even able to save back a hundred dollars for a leather jacket I had always wanted. What a blessing!

As the Lord continued to unlock this area of generosity I heard Him say, "Keith, I want to bless you, but if you do not receive my blessings for you then you won't be blessed." I assumed that the only way to financial blessing was the simple act of giving through tithes and offerings. The Lord said, "That is *one* of my Kingdom principles, but I am emphasizing something else in your life as well." I had always wondered why I didn't see blessing in my personal finances since I had practiced generosity throughout my life. The Lord said, "You have to learn to prosper your soul." He had me study 3 John 2 in the KJV. *"Beloved, I wish above all things that thou mayest prosper and be in health, even as thy soul prospereth."* This meant that to the extent that my soul prospered, my health and finances would naturally follow suit.

I often visited a fitness trail in the mountains surrounding the town in which I lived. It was called a *parcourse* and consisted of a trail equipped with obstacles or stations distributed along its length designed to provide a complete set of physical exercises. At the end of the course was a place where you could measure your blood pressure. As I walked the course one day the Lord downloaded, in complete detail, a "Soul Test" consisting of twenty questions designed to help determine the health of my life. It wasn't something I had to ponder — it came to me all at once. When I returned home, I typed out the test but did not take it for three days. I didn't even review it after writing it down because I was pretty sure I'd fail...miserably! Sure enough, when I finally took the test, I failed. The test revealed that I was not a well-balanced person. But, armed with the wisdom of 3 John 2, I determined to make some changes.

Above all else, I longed for a healthier marriage, but I had been so caught up in vocational ministry that I spent time or money pursuing it. Valentine's Day was around the corner and I wanted to surprise my wife with a weekend away.

Together.

Just the two of us.

No children allowed!

Within a day or so a friend called to offer reservations at a very plush hotel in a nearby city. With hot tubs and fireplaces in each room, it sounded like the perfect romantic getaway. In anticipation of the week's events, Heather and I browsed through a jewelry store looking at rings. She tried one on and her eyes lit up. Of course, she liked it. Sadly, I didn't have the hundred dollars to cover the cost.

Within a couple hours of our trip to the jewelry store, we spent some time with a prophetic mentor of ours. Just as we were leaving, he pulled me aside and placed one hundred dollars into my hand and said, "Just because." He knew nothing about the ring! What did I do? I went straight back to that store and bought the ring for Heather. Things were looking up. I had the ring; I had a nice hotel room reserved. Now, all I needed was some spending money. God is so great! That Sunday a friend at church gave me a few hundred dollars, which, for the record, I did *not* give away! Instead, I thanked the Lord, recognizing the Father's attempt to bless, foster and nurture our marriage. I realized that this was part of me getting "my soul prosperous" and taking care of my heart and the hearts of those I loved.

Truly learning to give from my heart and knowing when to receive entailed a great deal of work. For many years I had watched my parents generously give to others and because we lived in the parsonage adjacent to the church, transients frequently stopped by in search of help. Often there was nothing in the church to give, so the supplies of the pastor became the source of supply for the transients. When I began pastoring, I emulated my parents, assuming that I needed to be the generous benefactor regardless of circumstance. I gave constantly to people in our church, buying meals and supplying their needs. But something in my heart just did not feel right.

Basically, I didn't understand true generosity.

I once had a yellow bike. It was something my father had given me and it was something of great personal value. I ran across a young man who was in need of transportation, so I gave him that bike. My bike. My nice yellow bike! It was hard, but I did it out of a spirit of generosity. A few days later he showed up on my doorstep to inform me that the bike had been stolen. "Oh well, easy come, easy go," was his flippant comment in the face of the loss. I have to be honest with you...that really ticked me off! I had given him my special bike and he had not exhibited even the slightest bit of gratitude for my sacrifice.

Shortly after this, our church attended a movie together as a bonding experience. The individual coordinating the event phoned me the day of the movie alleging that he did not have enough money to buy tickets for his family, so they wouldn't be attending. I quickly offered to take care of their tickets. When I arrived at the theater and approached the ticket counter, all I had in my possession was a debit card...and the theater only accepted cash. The man, who was standing right behind me, proceeded to take out his wallet and produce enough cash to pay for their tickets — money that he supposedly didn't have. Once again, I was very upset. It seemed that even though the money had been there all along, he had allowed me to offer to pay his way.

Through these two incidents I sensed the Lord unwrapping the inner workings of my heart in relation to giving. "Keith, you give to many people but your heart is not truly in it." I always felt an *obligation* to give instead of a *joy* to give. It was a core value drilled into each one of us growing up: Give, give and give some more. The Lord allowed me to emerge from the bondage of giving out of obligation in order to unearth the pleasure of giving out of joy. 2 Corinthians 9:7 says, "*Each man should give what he has decided in his heart to give, not reluctantly or under compulsion, for God loves a cheerful giver.*" To have a truly free and healthy soul you must live life without obligation or false responsibility toward others. You must have the power to say "yes" on your own accord, instead of feeling pressured or forced into a decision. Religion attempts to shackle us to Biblical principles without being led by the Holy Spirit.

One afternoon as I was at home spending time with the Lord, there was a knock at the door. At the time we still lived next to the church. When I opened the door I saw a boy on crutches and girl standing by his side, both obviously transients. When they told me that they needed socks for their feet, I felt overwhelmed by God's love and led them to the church building where I found socks and shoes as well. Still feeling overwhelmed by God's love, I told the boy that I would pray for his feet feeling confident that God would heal him. So I prayed and he was healed. The young man walked out of the building without his crutches. They were both unbelievably touched. They had come seeking socks to cover their bare feet, but had gotten both socks *and* shoes along with physical healing. Later on, the girl returned to my home and confessed that prior to their encounter that day she had been an atheist. She said, "Now, I'm not so sure," and hugged me, thanking me for the kindness I had demonstrated to two total strangers.

Jesus said in Matthew 10:8, "...*Freely you have received, freely give.*" The love of God permeated me and the generosity of heaven had flowed through me resulting in changed lives. In John 15:12 Jesus says, "*My command is this: Love each other as I have loved you.*" In another passage, Mark 12:31, Jesus also says, "*'Love your neighbor as yourself.' There is no commandment greater than these.*" We cannot truly give anything away that we have not first received for ourselves. The Lord demonstrates benevolence toward us despite our mistakes, or even our unwise use of His resources. Romans 5:8, "*But God demonstrates his own love for us in this: While we were still sinners, Christ died for us.*" His abundant love must be received in every area of our lives if we are to have healthy souls. It is only when our souls become healthy that we are able to truly receive and give.

Ecclesiastes 4:8 says, *There was a man all alone; he had neither son nor brother. There was no end to his toil, yet his eyes were not content with his wealth. "For whom am I toiling," he asked, "and why am I depriving myself of enjoyment?" This too is meaningless — a miserable business!* I agree completely. If we are unable to enjoy our lives with the ones we love, we survive yet another day in misery. I had to learn how to give and receive, to enjoy life, find balance and take care of every area of my life through God's design. I found Ecclesiastes 5:19 to be very freeing. "*Moreover, when God gives any man wealth and possessions, and enables him to enjoy them, to accept his lot and be happy in his work — this is a gift of God.*"

God desires to give us a life that we enjoy, work that is fulfilling and an ability to take pleasure in every part of our human experience. This is God's gift to us. The original curse in Genesis was toil. Genesis 3:17-19 says, *To Adam he said, "Because you listened to your wife and ate from the tree about which I commanded you, 'You must not eat of it,' "Cursed is the ground because of you; through painful toil you will eat of it all the days of your life. It will produce thorns and thistles for you, and you will eat the plants of the field. By the sweat of your brow you will eat your food until you return to the ground, since from it you were taken; for dust you are and to dust you will return.*

Toil is joyless work and is a curse! Adam was created to walk intimately with the Father in the garden from a place of security and intimacy. His responsibility to work the land and nurture what God had given him wasn't hard labor, but simple pleasure. But when sin entered the world, toil came with it. Many people in the workforce despise their jobs. Their primary goal seems to be getting through the day; just hanging on for the weekend so they can "start living." People don't just need a sabbatical! They need a sabbatical *lifestyle*.

God does not just want good workers. He wants lovers who enjoy every part of creation. Matthew 7:22-23 says, *Many will say to me on that day, 'Lord, Lord, did we not prophesy in your name, and in your name drive out demons and perform many miracles?' Then I will tell them plainly, 'I never knew you. Away from me, you evildoers!'* Here, God refers to believers who went through the motions of principle-led Christianity without ever knowing the heart of God. The word, "knew" in this passage, is the Greek word *ginosko*: To know intimately. You did all these things for me, but you never knew me. Mark 8:36 says, *"What good is it for a man to gain the whole world, yet forfeit his soul?"* Normally, when we refer to this passage we are describing someone who gains vast wealth in this life, but is destined for hell. I would like to propose that you could gain the whole world, minister, faithfully serve God and enter heaven while never enjoying fullness of life and others in the process.

Part of the Lord's Prayer deals with this very topic. Matthew 6:13 says, "And lead us not into temptation, but deliver us from the evil one.'" The word translated "evil one" is the Greek word, *poneros*, which in its root form means, "toil." Jesus tells us to pray that we be delivered from the *toiler*. The devil is the one who strives to weigh us down under a work mentality: work, work, work.

Galatians 3:3 says, *"Are you so foolish? After beginning with the Spirit, are you now trying to attain your goal by human effort?"* 2 Peter 1:3 says, *"His divine power has given us everything we need for life and godliness through our knowledge of him who called us by his own glory and goodness."* In other words, we received everything we needed at the beginning. We did not earn it; it was freely given to us. Anything we gain through work, we will have to keep by work. Anything we receive by His good grace, we can give away at will.

Matthew 13:19 says, *"When anyone hears the message about the kingdom and does not understand it, the evil one comes and snatches away what was sown in his heart. This is the seed sown along the path."* The phrase "evil one" here is, once again, *poneros:* To toil. The message of the Kingdom is that our right standing with God produces joy and peace because of what He did. Failing to recognize that we entered the Kingdom through Jesus' life-giving sacrifice opens us to the lie of the enemy that says we must work for what has already been freely given. The promised land of our destiny must be received through rest...not toil. He wants to give freely what you have not sown through hard labor.

Let me share a final story.

During our first year in Vacaville, we directed the second year students of The Mission's Supernatural School of Ministry. We dreamt with our senior leaders about starting a ten-week school in Fiji where we would live while managing the program.

Heather and I finished up the first year in Vacaville and decided to go to Fiji with our family to get the ten-week school established there. This was our first experience at planting a school and we were thrilled. When we arrived, several of the Fijian ministers excitedly informed us about all the ministry experiences they had planned, the places we were going to travel as well as the desperate needs of the people. It didn't take long for us to realize that they planned to work us to exhaustion!

After hearing about all their plans, I had a dream from the Lord. In the dream, the Lord told me, "Keith, I selected Fiji because your wife wanted a place to enjoy her family. I do not want you spending all your time in vocational ministry. I want you to spend some of your time really enjoying your family there." Since I was still struggling to find a balance between spending time with my family and maintaining a passionate heart for the Body of Christ, this dream was very freeing.

We spent that summer in Fiji with our children, living in a rental house on one of the main islands. We led the school and invested many hours into making it a success. God was remarkably faithful and we experienced breakthrough after breakthrough. We escorted the students to many villages, other islands and churches. Everywhere we traveled we were filled with joy over witnessing countless healings and seeing our students prophesy over many people. With the help of locals and the support of The Mission, our ten weeks were extremely successful.

We worked hard, but we also played hard. When not in ministry, we could be found swimming in pools, snorkeling in the ocean, relaxing at beautiful resorts or experiencing a variety of family adventures. Often on our days off, our local administrator would call and I found it troubling to tell him that we were simply out enjoying ourselves. But God told me, "Keith, there is so much more to life than just ministry." It was difficult to honestly share our pleasurable pursuits because many of the Fijians were so poor. I thought more than once that to them it probably seemed like a huge waste of money to spend time abroad enjoying ourselves. We spent our entire savings that summer, but treasured our time together. And when we returned home, we had no regrets.

I posted our adventures on Facebook and, sadly, a few individuals left comments indicating that in their minds we did not minister at all... that it had simply been an extended vacation. We must understand that God is pleased when our ministry encompasses enjoying loved ones and pursuing personal desires and dreams. In spite of having grown up in a paradigm that said true ministry required pain and sacrifice...we found a way to enjoy ourselves. Had we not done so, we would not have made it through that summer. We poured ourselves into the school each and every week, helping to bring those students into a Kingdom revelation that many of them had never experienced. It was well worth the fight.

As I bring this chapter — this book — to a close, I would like to leave you with the previously mentioned *Soul Test*. My prayer is that you will truly prosper as your soul prospers. Refuse to be a "one-hit wonder!" Refuse to be someone who sprints a hundred yards and burns out. I have observed far too many casualties in life: People who achieved success in a variety of areas, only to later discover their marriage was not intact, their financial status fraudulent or their children's well-being in shambles.

My desire is that you strive to become an endurance athlete in Christ, excelling in all God has called you to be in this race called life.

May you thoroughly enjoy every part of the journey, from the starting line to the finish.

May you smell the roses along the way.

May you truly be captivated by every part of His expanding Kingdom.

I have found that there is more...more than I ever dreamed. You can find the *more* of God as well. Accept nothing less!

May you be blessed; may you learn to enjoy to the fullest everything God has created; and may you experience life that is more than you could ever think or imagine.

Soul Test

Scoring: There is a total of 100 points. Give yourself 1-5 points based on how you answer each question.

5- I am healthy in this area.

4- I am doing well in this area, but could do a little better.

3- I am doing okay in this area, but need some work to improve here

2- I am not doing well in this area at all. I'd better seriously look at what I can do to improve here.

1- I am doing terrible in this area. I need help to start a healthy habit in this area.

Part 1 – Physical Health

- Do I set aside quality time for my body on a regular basis? (Example: Do I exercise at least thirty minutes three times per week?)____

- Do I get seven to nine hours of sleep per night? _____

- Do I eat a healthy meal at least 5 times per week?_____

- Do I drink at least six to eight glasses of water per day?____

- Do I take one day off every week as a day to rest and relax, enjoy family and friends? ____

- Do I have a personal hobby, enjoyment or activity that I pursue on a weekly basis? _____

- Do I get away once a month from my normal living environment? Do I get out of town and away from my normal job, home or setting to enjoy a new perspective on life?____

Part 2 – Relational Health

- Do I have a healthy relationship with my spouse? Do we spend at least one evening a week in quality time together? If you do not have a spouse, is there a significant friend in your life with whom you spend quality time? ____

- Do I have a healthy relationship with two other people besides my spouse? (Example: Do I hang out, talk, enjoy or have fun once or twice a month with a friend?) ____

- On a monthly basis do I have a person in my life who mentors me? ___

- On a monthly basis do I have a person in my life whom I mentor? ____

- Do I have time for myself, or do I have so many things going on in my life helping others that I have no time for myself?____

- Do I have time for others, or do I have so many personal things going on in my life that I have no time for others?____

Part 3 – Emotional health

- Do I walk in a lifestyle of joy and happiness? Do I find myself laughing and smiling often, for no apparent reason? ____

- Do I walk in a lifestyle of peace? Do I carry a light load or am I constantly weighed down with the cares of life, finances, relationships or prayer agendas that life brings my way?____

- Do I walk in a lifestyle of love? Do I have grace and mercy for others' shortcomings or do I find myself critical, impatient, irritated or offended with people? ____

- Do I enjoy the blessings God gives? (Example: Do I give away all the money, gifts and time that comes my way to meet the needs of others, or do I feel deserving of enjoying His blessings?)____

Part 4 – Devotional health

- On a daily basis do I have praise and thanks leaving my lips for the goodness of God? Is the praise and thanks mechanical or heartfelt? _____

- Do I get quality time with Jesus regularly? Do I spend time edifying my soul through my heavenly language, soaking music, prayer or Bible reading? _____

- Do I get built up spiritually in a group setting at least 6-8 times a month? Church meetings, home fellowships. _____

Score

     Part 1_____
     Part 2_____
     Part 3_____
     Part 4_____
     Total _____

95-100 – You are doing splendidly. Keep it up.

90-95 – Well done. You are healthy. Just top off your gas for a full tank.

85-90 – You are doing well. Pay attention to areas that need help.

80-85 – Your health is in need of attention. Do not gain the world and lose your soul.

75-80 – You are living a manageable life, but you are hurting. You can benefit from spending quality time on areas that need improvement.

75 and below – Seriously look at areas needing help. You are on your way to burnout if you are not already there. You need to spend several months developing healthy habits.

Epilogue

The following dream illustrates what the *more* looks like and is a concise picture of what the Lord is causing His bride to rise up and become.

My Dream for the Church

I dream of a bride that is equal in every way to Christ because they truly see Christ as He is; risen and seated at the right hand of God.

I dream of a bride that truly knows God's voice for themselves and are no longer unhealthily dependent on another's ability to hear God.

I dream of a bride that has been fully captured by the revelation of His love; a bride that knows and responds to His presence in every situation because they value and honor Him above all else.

I dream of a thankful bride, a worshiping bride, a dancing, shouting, praising bride, who knows how to celebrate freely and wildly the goodness of God in every situation, unashamed of their love and devotion towards the King.

I dream of a bride that is in healthy relationships with one another, not divided, bitter, jealous or masked, but a bride who is authentic, truthful and loving toward each other.

I dream of a bride that doesn't relate to others on the basis of race, class, status, church affiliations, upbringings, doctrinal similarities, failures or successes, but relates to each other out of the revelation that they are all one in Christ and have one Father who is Lord and God of all.

I dream of a resting bride, free of toil, not working for the machine of religion but enjoying life, God, family and friends; and out of that place advancing the Kingdom of God in every realm of their life as they walk in their identities as beloved children in whom He is well-pleased.

I dream of a bride who is free of poverty, lack and feelings of inferiority and helplessness. A bride who knows they are sons and daughters of the King, people of royalty, people of wealth, generous in every situation, so that no one is lacking.

I dream of a bride who lives out of the revelation that they are a spirit being living in a temporary human body, living from heavenly reality towards every situation they face on earth, walking in every heavenly gift, partnering with the angels and God who is Spirit.

I dream of a bride full of freedom, full of truth, living in the light, able to transparently live their lives in front of people.

I dream of a bride who knows their true identity and purpose for being alive and from that place of identity pursues the dreams of their hearts and the fullness of their promise land.

I dream of a bride that brings the fullness of His power into every realm demonstrating the superiority of Christ's finished work over the devil, displaying His awesome power, His answers for difficult situations, His interpretations and solutions to the dreams of the pharaohs of this world. A bride walking in the overcoming authority of Christ.

I dream of the bride invading every kingdom of this world including government, business, media, school, music, art, sports, etc. and walking in the authority of Christ to make the Kingdoms of this world the Kingdoms of our God bringing the return of the King.

END

About the Author

Keith is a third generation pastor who now travels internationally speaking in churches, conferences, ministry schools and other venues. Keith carries a message of freedom for the body of Christ helping the church move into a Kingdom culture. He is a prophetic voice who carries a breaker anointing to open up the heavens and bring timely corporate and personal prophetic words and life transforming teaching. Keith is passionate to see the fullness of heaven's atmosphere here on earth and bring people into heavenly encounters through encounter events, impartation and signs and wonders.

Keith and his wife Heather spent ten years as the Senior Leaders at Shiloh Gateway of Worship in Willits California where they walked out what they teach and impart. Over the past several years they have overseen, planted and worked with a variety of ministry schools in the United States and internationally. They carry a strong anointing to break the heavens open over churches, regions and nations through presence based ministry, prophetic teaching and impartation. They have traveled to many nations bringing people into radical encounters with God. People experience freedom, deliverance, healing and the love of God in their meetings.

To find out more about Keith and Heather, you can check out their website at www.ferranteministries.com. If you're interested in inviting Keith to minister, you can e-mail him at:

keith@ferranteministries.com.